T0343130

JIMMY CARTER

JIMMY CARTER
THE LAST INTERVIEW
and OTHER CONVERSATIONS

MELVILLE HOUSE
BROOKLYN · LONDON

JIMMY CARTER: THE LAST INTERVIEW
AND OTHER CONVERSATIONS

Copyright © 2023 by Melville House Publishing

Firing Line with William F. Buckley Jr., April 23, 1973, copyright by the Hoover Institution, Hoover Institution Library & Archives, container 800040.

"Jimmy, We Hardly Know Y'All" © 1976 by *Playboy* Magazine. All rights reserved. First published in *Playboy*, November 1976.

"Debating Our Destiny," Jim Lehrer, *PBS NewsHour*, April 28, 1989. Copyright © 1989 by Public Broadcasting System.

"Cold War: Backyard" used by permission of the National Security Archive at George Washington University, which provided essential research and primary sources for the CNN Cold War series. https://nsarchive2.gwu.edu/coldwar/interviews/episode-18/carter1.html

"The Gospel According to Jimmy," *GQ* magazine, © 2005 by Condé Nast.

"On Civil Rights and Justice," interview by Derreck Kayongo, C-SPAN, May 20, 2016. © 2016 by C-SPAN.

"Celebrating with the Carters," interview with Judy Woodruff, PBS, July 5, 2021. Used by permission. All rights reserved.

First Melville House printing: February 2024

Melville House Publishing   Suite 2000
            46 John Street and 16/18 Woodford Road
Brooklyn, NY 11201   London E7 0HA

mhpbooks.com
@melvillehouse

ISBN: 978-1-61219-152-7
ISBN: 978-1-61219-153-4 (EBOOK)

Printed in the United States of America
1 3 5 7 9 10 8 6 4 2

A catalog record for this book is available from the Library of Congress.

The authorized representative in the EU for product safety and compliance is Easy Access System Europe, Mustamäe tee 50, 10621 Tallinn, Estonia. gpsr.requests@easproject.com

CONTENTS

JIMMY CARTER

FIRING LINE

INTERVIEW BY WILLIAM F. BUCKLEY JR.
FIRING LINE
APRIL 23, 1973

WILLIAM F. BUCKLEY JR.: Ladies and gentlemen, I apologize to Governor Carter for very briefly deferring the scheduled discussion. I do this to report on the future of *Firing Line*. As many of you know, the Corporation for Public Broadcasting declined to make a grant to continue the program for reasons it was at pains to state had no bearing on the quality of the program. At their meeting two weeks ago, the corporation failed to reach agreement concerning alternative means of financing. Accordingly, we shall attempt during the next fortnight to syndicate *Firing Line* by offering it to every public television station for the ensuing season. If the stations are able to respond, we shall continue on the air. If not, this will be the penultimate program of *Firing Line*, unless Governor Carter wants to invoke the doctrine of interposition.

James Earl Carter Jr. startled the country and possibly even some of his constituents by opening his inaugural address as governor of Georgia with the statement, "I say to you quite frankly that the time for racial discrimination is over." Considering that the governor's predecessor was Lester Maddox and that there was no revolution between the end of his predecessor's term and the beginning of his own, the transition was a remarkable feat of social history. Governor

Carter simply doesn't spend much time nowadays talking about racial problems. It is his thesis that southern governors nowadays face other problems much the same as those faced by governors of states outside the South. The evolution of welfare policies is one example. Jimmy Carter was born in Georgia, attended briefly the Georgia Institute of Technology, and went to the United States Naval Academy at Annapolis. He intended to make a career in the Navy, but when his father died, he retired from atomic submarines and in 1953 began a career as a peanut farmer and warehouse operator in which he prospered. He went to the Georgia Senate in 1962 and began his long campaign for governor in 1969. He is a Baptist of firm conviction. Although the economic situation in Georgia is greatly encouraging, it has its slums and its welfare problems, and Governor Carter, like everyone else, has ideas on many subjects, including the subject of welfare reform. Just to get a little perspective, I shall like to begin by asking Governor Carter whether he thinks his fellow Democrat Senator George McGovern made constructive welfare proposals during the campaign last year.

JIMMY CARTER: No, I don't believe so. If it was intended to be constructive, I don't think it was accepted constructively by the American people. I thought it was a terrible mistake for the Democrats to nominate George McGovern, although I think his heart was probably in the right place. About a year ago, I started a campaign, among the governors at least, to tell them about the devastating consequences of nominating Senator McGovern. I think that his own proposal at that time to have a guaranteed minimum wage, I mean, a guaranteed minimum annual income, was very similar to what President Nixon proposed from Mr. Moynihan. But the Congress was not in a proper attitude to add 17 million new welfare recipients as would have been required with Mr. Nixon's program, and neither were they nor the American people willing to put everyone in the nation on a $1,000-a-year gift from the welfare program as proposed by Senator McGovern. This is a complicated mechanism that is extremely necessary, building lives of many people who are dependent on it, but which has very little support from among the majority of Americans who are able to work for a living and who have the inclination to work for a living.

BUCKLEY: Well, but your recommendations are presumably not based, at least not exclusively, on what it is that the American people want. As a governor, you occasionally feel surely the [*inaudible*] is to tell them what they ought to want. Now, ought they to want a guaranteed annual wage?

CARTER: I don't think so. I've been extremely critical recently of President Nixon's . . .

BUCKLEY: . . . role in Watergate?

CARTER: Well, as a Democrat, that's been some interesting news for me, but I hope they don't involve President Nixon personally. I think it'll be a blow to the nation. But I think his extremely misleading attitude toward revenue sharing where he takes money to give to local and state governments under the guise of wealth [and] of revenue sharing and all of the money comes from the people who are all legitimately dependent upon the government to help them overcome some sort of an affliction. In Georgia, we don't have any welfare program for able-bodied men at all, and the only able-bodied women who can qualify for welfare are those who have dependent children. I might say that for a woman with four children, maximum payments are about a dollar a day per person, which is certainly no bed of roses. But President Nixon has in his latest rulings, through Mr. Weinberger, done away with an option that a woman of this sort has who may have been on welfare for all of her life and who now can put her kids in a daycare center, get a job. But if she makes the minimum wage, then according to the latest rulings of Mr. Weinberger and the HEW [Health, Education, and Welfare] department, she's no longer qualified to put her kids in a daycare center. This is a kind of obvious conflict that I see. I think that the welfare program ought to be designed specifically for two reasons. One, to give a modicum, really, of human dignity to a blind person or an afflicted person or one who's too old to support himself. On the other hand, to be designed to help able[d] people overcome handicaps of training or race or education or economic and social background enough to become self-sufficient. But quite often in recent months, the policies of the federal government has been to attenuate this trend in the welfare programs, and we take a very conservative attitude toward welfare in Georgia. We don't have the fancy additional allocations of funds, but I do think that we ought to provide food, clothing, housing for people who can't afford it, and a chance to be self-sufficient for those who are able to.

BUCKLEY: Speaking of self-sufficiency and of the enormous progress, economic progress, in Georgia in the last few years, how close to self-sufficiency is Georgia in terms of federal welfare? I define self-sufficiency as the state that sends in tax dollars to Washington about as much as it gets in tax dollars back from Washington. You're still below that level, aren't you?

CARTER: Yes, we are. Each year since the welfare program has started, Georgia's percentage of contribution to the basic program has increased. This past year we jumped, I believe, from 29 percent to 31.5 percent, which means that the state is more economically able to pay an additional cost than it was before, but we still receive more back total from the federal government than we pay in taxes.

BUCKLEY: Now, explain to me how it works. As I understand it, federal welfare money is geared to a scale that is substantially set by the state itself so that if you have a fairly parsimonious or frugal or careful, if you like, welfare policy, then that which you qualify for from the federal government is accordingly shaped. Is that correct?

CARTER: That's right. We are slightly above the minimum federal levels in the state. In the past we have been, I think, exactly at a dollar per day per person for a mother and four children, which is the most controversial part of the program, the aid for families with dependent children, and we've only gone a half dollar perhaps for the five of them beyond that point, so we are, as you say, careful or parsimonious in our allocation of state funds, and of that portion, the federal government pays a little less than 70 percent. The state government pays a little bit more than 30 percent. The new federal proposals, as you know, the HEW in Washington will take over the responsibility for the social security aspects of it to care for the aged, the blind, and the totally disabled, and the states will continue to administer the program for the dependents, mothers whose husbands either are unknown or have left the family and the home. Another part of the program that is of great concern to all of us is that there is no present program whatsoever for an underemployed person, for someone who really tries to earn a living. It may be a mother who has part-time work as a maid in a home or as an LPN [licensed practical nurse] or some other thing like that. But there is no allocation of funds now for a person who does have a partial income, and it discourages initiative on the part of many, and it also encourages fathers who are unknown to deliberately leave their families in order to let the rest of their family qualify for welfare assistance. I think those are two of the items in welfare that need to be corrected.

BUCKLEY: But isn't it predictable that the Democratic Party, having moved substantially in that direction anyway, is going to be calling at the next national convention for a guaranteed annual wage? Now to what extent is a Democrat whose inclinations would probably be judged as rather atavistic by some of your northern colleagues, to what extent do you feel bound by the deliberations of the National Democratic Party? Or is it your feeling that this is really a loose alliance and that your use of the word "Democrat" has to be tailored to local conditions?

CARTER: Well, I would defy anybody to discern the attitude of a Democratic Party, and I think "loosely bound" is a very loose expression for something that's much looser than you can describe in words. There is no way to describe a Democratic Party policy on welfare. I think, however, that even the most conservative democratic leaders of the past, Senator Walter George, for instance, and Senator Dick Russell of Georgia, have always taken a posture that a legitimate function of government is to deal with inherent afflictions of people. Senator George considered his greatest contribution to the nation's welfare, although he was chairman of the Foreign Affairs Committee, he considered his greatest contribution the evolution of federal aid to education in the form of career or technical education, and he wrote the landmark bill that's still in effect there. Senator Russell told me shortly before he died that he thought the best contribution that he had ever made was to evolve a free lunchroom program for poor children. I think that southern politicians, statesmen, no matter how conservative they might be in their general reputation, have always felt that one of the prime functions of government was to discern the afflictions of a citizen and try to help them overcome it, whether it was retardation in case of a mentally afflicted person or a lack of education in case of Senator George, a lack of adequate diet in case of Senator Russell's school lunchroom program, or in the welfare program, to give a helpless person enough money to live on. This might be a southern characteristic, but they've always been very cautious in it, and I think they've always tried to make sure that the contribution to a person was adequately repaid if the person was able to repay it. Senator

George, to train a person to hold a job. We have in Georgia an extremely rigid religious attitude toward a person's work ethic. It's hard to express in words, but the average Georgian feels that if he doesn't do a day's work for a day's pay, he somehow violated his religious conscience, and we have because of that, eager applicants for jobs in the state. We have practically a nonexistent—

BUCKLEY: In the North, we call that the Puritan ethic.

CARTER: Puritan ethic. Well, we have a similar one. We live in the Bible Belt and that's part of it. But we have an unemployment rate in the state of about 3.5 percent, sometimes ranging less, and this includes, obviously, students who are not in college, women who worked part-time and who have worked in the past and so forth. But I believe that we consider the welfare program to be part of a manpower development program or part of an industry recruitment program, part of a technical school or career school program, all designed to help people stand on their own feet, to develop their own individuality, to be self-sufficient, and to play a role in government, and this is the way I look at it. I think that the average welfare recipient in Georgia, if given a chance, will take training and will hold a job. We've had this proven in a few instances. I can recall one community in the state—Griffin, Georgia, down just south of Atlanta about forty miles—where they had a large influx a few years back of textile industry, and we had a fairly high welfare role and a training program was put into it, and almost all of the women who had children at home who were receiving welfare volunteered to take a training program and went to work. But, well, I think you can see that if you are a mother and you love your children and you see your child perhaps doomed to spending the rest of its childhood life, at least, trying to pay for food, clothing, housing, medicine, school supplies, and so forth on a dollar per day, that just the natural love of a mother for a child will induce her to seek better things for her family. I believe that the welfare program is obviously necessary. We need to avoid the restraints that prevents somebody from receiving welfare payments if they do try to help themselves, and we need to emphasize that the training and job qualification aspects of the program, which hasn't been done in the past.

BUCKLEY: Well, do you think it's possible to say that southern history and southern culture has resulted in an attitude towards welfare that is in any way distinctive from the attitude in other states? Could it be that you feel in the South an avuncular relationship that was distilled out of your experience with slavery, which now gets transformed to a feeling of responsibility for people irrespective of their color who need help of that kind? Is that different from the kind of thing that would be experienced in Maine or Oregon?

CARTER: Well, I couldn't judge the rest of the nation. I think that in the past, the obvious misconceptions of the welfare program have been based to some degree on racial thought that the welfare program was primarily designed for worthless citizens who didn't want to support themselves. But the fact of the matter is that this is not the case. As I said earlier, there is no program for able-bodied men, Black or white. I think another thing that's been obvious in the past is that the South, following the war between the states, did have a great need for gainful employment. We had a lot of small farms, and as the farms were mechanized, there was a choice to be made that—and I think we made the right choice in retrospect. One choice was to move into Atlanta, or to Chicago or to New York, and leave the farms and start a new life. A lot of the life, as you know, in New York and other places is based on a welfare recipient role for the rest of one's existence. In Georgia, and in many other states and some other states in the South, the people decided to stay at home and there was a major effort made and still is being made to locate small businesses, small manufacturing firms, close to the farm area, which can employ a person who doesn't have any high degree of education nor technological training but who's willing to work and able to work well with his hands. For instance, we've got a fine textile manufacturing complex in Georgia, and recently we've developed to the nation's foremost producer of mobile homes, a fairly high-paying job, but where the assembly of the mobile homes is done by hand labor, and the person who's lived his life on the farm can do this naturally without training.

BUCKLEY: These are the sales of non-Georgians, the mobile homes, right?

CARTER: And Georgians. And Georgians, sure.

BUCKLEY: Except they always stay at home.

CARTER: That's right. But so, instead of moving to Atlanta and living in a twenty-story-high apartment complex, they stay at home and live in the mobile home that they perhaps helped to construct. But we haven't had the masses move off the farm areas into the cities that other states have.

BUCKLEY: Well, is Georgia to be distinguished from other parts of the South as not having fed in any way the great migration of Black people to the northern and midwestern cities?

CARTER: No, we fed it. We fed it for a good period of time that I think ended eight or ten years ago. There was a migration out of the South. But now, as I say, our unemployment rate in Georgia is 3.5 percent, which is almost zero. We have a training program, for instance, founded on Mr. George's legislation whereby if any industry wants to come into a town in Georgia, we'll take their prospective employees, we'll help them select them, we'll recruit them, we'll screen them, and we'll actually train those employees so that the day the plant opens to manufacture whatever, those employees are ready to go to work already trained on the new plant's own machines, and there is a very fine interrelationship in Georgia between labor and management, regardless of whether the labor force might be a member of the union or not. I had an executive vice president of one of the major firms down in Georgia the other day who manufactures chewing gum. He had opened a small plant just south of Gainesville, Georgia. Two years ago, he had originally had two hundred employees. He told me that [of] all the two hundred original employees, after more than two years' time, he still had only lost five of them. He still had 195 and he had less than a 1 percent absentee rate. I think there's an embarrassment, first of all, about receiving welfare. There's a religious belief, as you say, the Puritan ethic, that causes a person to want to work and support himself, and there's a natural conservative attitude among the policy-makers of the state that hasn't created an attractive well for our program that would keep people from working if they can. But as I say, there are two basic defects in it that I've described earlier.

BUCKLEY: I know somebody who ran for your office a while back and says he was beaten primarily because he took a theoretical stand against the minimum wage and his position was orthodox as far as economists are concerned. That is to say, you can't find an economist who backs the idea of a minimum wage as an economically defensible proposition. To what extent have you found that nationally imposed minimum wage will retard economic development in your state?

CARTER: I don't think it has.

BUCKLEY: How come?

CARTER: Well, I have a vague memory of the first minimum wage proposal that the Democrats put forward that was opposed by the Republicans to establish a twenty-five-cents-an-hour guaranteed payment. When I finished high school, I got my first job off the farm working for the federal government measuring land for farmers, and it paid a forty-cent minimum wage, but I had to furnish my own automobile within the forty-cent allotment. Every time a minimum wage has been proposed, even beginning with this twenty-five-cent payment, it's been characterized by many of our southern statesmen officeholders as a blow against the South. But I think we've passed a point now where the influx of industry to provide jobs for our people is based on cheap labor, or on artificially contrived tax incentives, or on deterioration of the environment, and I believe that we are competitive now. We are shifting in our employment habits and our employment achievements from a bare minimum wage structure where that was a great escalation of what you had received in the past to one that's based on technology and advanced training. I think we're probably forty or fifty years behind, in some ways, the northeastern part of the United States, but we're moving rapidly.

BUCKLEY: Yeah, you're forty, fifty years ahead in some, too.

CARTER: In some, I agree.

BUCKLEY: Well, what you're really seeing, as I understand it, is the minimum wage doesn't really hurt you because most people are earning it as a matter of raw economic circumstances. But if you were the governor, say of Puerto Rico, you would probably be opposed to the minimum wage on the grounds that it is an unemployment-making social institution.

CARTER: I don't believe that I would, but I can certainly see arguments on both sides. My own belief is based on experience where every time we've had dire predictions of catastrophe if a minimum wage was established, and I've seen it come into a Georgia rural community where there was just one textile industry there that was owned by the most prominent family in the community who probably already owned, also owned, the bank, the Chevrolet dealership, and everything else in the town, and the advent of the minimum wage was predicted as completely destroying the town, but it hasn't. Now we've seen interlocking ownership of manufacturing plants, both in the textile field and many others, where a nationwide salary structure would greatly escalate the salary base in a given southern town. When that company put a plant in, it might automatically raise the average salary level for our employees, say a dollar an hour immediately when that new plant came in, and I've never seen a town suffer from it. I've never seen a community's economic structure suffer. In my opinion, it's always benefited when the average wage for the working people increased.

BUCKLEY: Well, it obviously does, assuming that there's an inflexible demand for the product. But when, for instance, they passed minimum wage in Chicago and within a year twenty-five thousand people who ran elevators for a living found that they were out of a job because elevators were automated, that's a pretty concrete result of a minimum wage. I take it that the situation in Georgia is one of those felicitous ones in which a high and rather vigorous upward-tending economy stays ahead of a minimum wage, that the minimum wage never acts, as I say, as an agent of unemployment.

CARTER: No, I didn't say that. I think quite often the minimum wage has acted to substantially influence beneficently, I think, the level of wages paid. I don't know whether it's true or—

BUCKLEY: If it were that simple, why don't we tell the Indians about it? There they work for twenty cents a day, not because they want to work for twenty cents a day. They'd much rather work for two dollars and twenty cents a day.

CARTER: But we are talking about a level of wages that actually is minimal in nature compared to the prevailing wage rates on the average around the nation. I don't think we've ever seen Congress, who are very conservative in this area, [pass] minimum wage rates above the average wages paid in the nation already.

BUCKLEY: Average has nothing to do with it. Certainly not average. But we're talking about the least, the people who are least able to cope competitively in the economy. The classic example is Black teenagers whose unemployment went up 100 percent after the minimum wage hike of the late 1950s. Now, maybe your point is "let's go ahead and victimize them because there are other discernible benefits of the noneconomic kind," but at least let's acknowledge that they're victims, right?

CARTER: Well, if you assume that elevators were automated because of the minimum wage.

BUCKLEY: I do. That's what they said.

CARTER: Well, my own belief would be that elevators would probably have been automated without the minimum wage. But based on that assumption, I think you can certainly build a good case. But as I say, I don't think that I've seen any impact, any adverse impact, in my own experience of establishment of minimum wages in the neighborhood that we've now witnessed of less than two dollars per hour.

BUCKLEY: Why would there be an unemployment rate of 3.2 in Georgia and an unemployment rate of 10 to 11 percent in New York City, given the fact that communications facilities between the two places are pretty effective? Why don't people leave New York where they don't work in order to go to Georgia where you can work?

CARTER: Well, I think that, as you know, the minimum wage is the same in both states, I presume, is it not?

BUCKLEY: Yeah.

CARTER: Well, I think that the average wage rate in New York is undoubtedly higher than Georgia. Also, there's a very attractive welfare program in New York, I understand, where people can make a substantial income without working. This is not the case in Georgia.

BUCKLEY: You do think that is a factor? It might have been a factor, for instance, in the emigration of the 1950s.

CARTER: The welfare programs?

BUCKLEY: Yeah.

CARTER: Yes, sir. I do. But I don't think the minimum wage was directly involved in it.

BUCKLEY: Do you have a residence requirement in Georgia?

CARTER: Yes.

BUCKLEY: A constitutional one?

CARTER: I think it's being challenged.

BUCKLEY: I see. Mr. Richard Skinner is an instructor of history at the University of South Carolina. Mr. Skinner?

RICHARD SKINNER: Governor Carter, I was interested, gathering from your comments about federal revenue sharing, what will be the effect of federal revenue sharing on your social welfare programs in Georgia?

CARTER: The revenue-sharing impact on Georgia has been all negative. We've seen, for instance, an allocation of revenue-sharing funds to the state that amounts to $36.6 million a year. We've had direct losses of federal funds that come through our state budget of $54 million with another $120 million in cutbacks in the state for other things that don't come through our state budget, like the construction of low-income housing and payments to farmers and so forth. Economically, it's been a blow to the state. The most insidious thing though about the revenue-sharing proposals has been that, although President Nixon and former Secretary of Treasury Connally assured the mayors and governors that revenue sharing would not be financed out of existing programs, that is exactly what has happened, and we've seen—

BUCKLEY: You mean financed by deducting from existing programs?

CARTER: Right, by deducting from existing programs, and the deductions have come from among the people who need the federal funds the most, the retarded children, the student loan program, the payments through the Title IV-A programs for mothers who leave their kids in daycare centers, for farm disaster programs. The reason this has come this way is that the federal programs in the field of social and educational effort have been designed historically, ever since I guess the time of Roosevelt or before, to fill gaps that existed among programs devised by local and state governments. Quite often, obviously, those gaps were the ones that provided for the poor or the defenseless or the non-influential, quite often the Black.

BUCKLEY: Why quite obviously? Why quite obviously?

CARTER: Well, because the local and state governments have almost always been orienting their programs toward the average or the middle-class person or one with—

BUCKLEY: Why should state officials be less altruistic than federal officials?

CARTER: Well, I think state and local officials both have some handicap in seeing things as a broad picture, and also there's a practical aspect of the effort that works against the poor because take your Title IV-A programs, the welfare payments, the daycare centers, the programs for retarded children, all of those, just because of the description of them, are designed for the poor. Well now, if the federal government takes the same amount of money and gives it to a state legislature and says, "All right. You take this money, and you spend it as you see fit," the natural human inclination is to divide that money at least equally among all of its people. They say, "We'll give the poor so much, the rich so much, and we'll build some golf courses. We'll give some tax refunds and so forth," and the money is coming from the poor programs, programs for the poor, and even in the most benevolent circumstances among the state legislature, the money's going to be oriented toward treating all the people of the state the same, so it's being taken from the poor and at best divided equally among all the people.

BUCKLEY: Yeah. I think it's rather an interesting generality that you're making that the further removed you are from a retarded child, the more likely you are to pity him. Why would that be so?

CARTER: Well—

BUCKLEY: I should think that a state legislature would be much more concerned over the distinct social problems in its state than you could ever expect a rather aloof government in Washington to be.

CARTER: Well, in the case of a retarded child, I think you'd be right. But in the special education programs, the Title I and Title III, the Title IV programs and others, these were designed specifically for the economically handicapped children. They're administered by state education departments, but they're designed for experimental purposes. The Head Start program is designed with a limitation on economic income for the family [of] the child to qualify. The same thing applies, of course, with the welfare program, with your manpower training programs. These programs that are designed to help a person become self-sufficient or to receive some compensatory education naturally accrued to the people who can't finance it themselves or who can't go to a private school or who can't go to a private sanitarium for treatment, so the nationwide programs in the field of health or education or welfare or labor are naturally designed for the poorer people.

BUCKLEY: Well, let's just go on to Ms. Margaret Young, who's an instructor in foreign languages at the University of South Carolina.

MARGARET YOUNG: Governor Carter, since most people on welfare are women, do you see the welfare problem as related to other problems women face in our society such as job discrimination, childcare, exclusion from decision-making positions in most institutions?

BUCKLEY: In fact, they're mostly children, aren't they? Rather than women?

YOUNG: Well, this—

CARTER: Women with dependent children.

YOUNG: It's aid to families—

BUCKLEY: But it's aid to the children via the mother, right?

CARTER: Right.

YOUNG: In effect. But it's the women who are heads of the families that are receiving the money.

BUCKLEY: It's the women who bred the children.

YOUNG: That's true.

BUCKLEY: That's part of that inequality.

CARTER: That's right. I doubt if we could change that circumstance, that the women are the ones who produce the children, but as you know—

BUCKLEY: George McGovern forgot to change that one.

CARTER: But I think it is obviously the case that the welfare program has been designed by Congress and has always been administered, so far as I can remember, is designed to provide funds for a mother with children only if her husband, common-law husband or official husband, has departed, either dead or has left the family. Quite often this departure is a subterfuge. The husband might be lurking in the background waiting for the welfare supervisor to look the other way. But it has prevented the family from being reconstituted if the father is present.

BUCKLEY: It's atomizing.

CARTER: It is.

BUCKLEY: Why don't they change that? I've never heard anybody in my entire life defend this thing, and for some reason, it doesn't ever get changed.

CARTER: I know. I think the reason for it is that there's a hang-up against paying any sort of welfare payments to a man who's physically capable of working, so the Congress apparently has just simply said, "Well, this man doesn't exist as far as his children are concerned," and they're requiring legally that he not exist as far as the welfare supervisor's concerned, so in effect he's wiped out of the family picture by law, and in order for his family to qualify for the very minimal welfare payments available, he has to be absent from the home. There is also a prohibition in the welfare program of making a payment to supplement wages earned by a head of the household. If a person goes to work and earns a minimum wage, there is no provision under the law for that person's income to be supplemented by a welfare payment. The most recent ruling of the title under the Title IV-A program has further exacerbated this particular instance, whereby I described a welfare mother who can now leave her kids in a Title IV-A daycare center if she earns a minimum wage is by definition or regulation disqualified from leaving her kid in the welfare center any longer, so she honestly has only one choice. She has to take her kid out of the daycare center, back home, and go back on welfare. We've had this—

BUCKLEY: You mean if she earns the minimum wage for forty hours a week, right? You don't mean if she earns the minimum wage but has only part-time work?

CARTER: No. If she earns a minimum wage for forty hours a week, yes.

BUCKLEY: Well, might they be trying to say that people who earn the minimum wage ought not to be burdened on other people who are merely earning the minimum wage, and since any archeology done on the collection of dollars shows that quite poor people are paying very considerable taxes, there's an attempt there, isn't there, at rough economic justice?

CARTER: It would be rough.

BUCKLEY: Well, why should you tax—

CARTER: It would be rough.

BUCKLEY: Yeah.

CARTER: Rough economic justice because a mother with four children whose earning say $2,500 a year would not pay any income tax.

BUCKLEY: Well, she's getting relief from that, at that level, as opposed to a woman who had no children would be paying tax.

CARTER: That's right. That's right. There's another very peculiar ruling that I can't understand that President Nixon or Mr. Weinberger has promulgated, and that is that in the 75/25 matching formula in the Title IV-A, if the local people have raised the money privately, if a group of mothers who have, say the retarded kids we had mentioned earlier, have raised this money with cake sales or with basketball games or by public subscription, then they cannot any longer use that privately raised money to match the 75 percent that comes from the federal government and those locally initiated.

BUCKLEY: It's got to be state tax money to qualify for the 75.

CARTER: It's got to all be, yes. Now in Georgia, because we don't have—

BUCKLEY: It doesn't sound very Nixon-ish, does it? I mean, he'd be very much in favor of cake sales. Well, so am I. So am I.

CARTER: Apparently, he isn't, though, because this is the regulation that was promulgated by the Health, Education, and Welfare Department this past January. If any portion of the local matching fund comes from private sources, you can't qualify for the federal funds.

BUCKLEY: Is this a way of trying to discipline the states, saying to the states, "We don't count it as you doing your effort if, in fact, you are not doing it, but you are requiring, you are using the private ingenuity of people to do it for you." Is this the thinking behind that?

CARTER: I honestly can't understand the motivation of it. Mr. Colucci, who was formerly the head of the OEO [Office of Economic Opportunity] program, who then went through the Office—

BUCKLEY: Came up with it?

CARTER: —Office of Management and Budget, and then he wound up in HEW, so I guess that OMB experience maybe changed his attitude. But this has been the case. I don't think it's a matter of disciplining the states because most of these particular programs are direct contractual arrangements between the local community itself and the federal law agency.

BUCKLEY: Well, then in that case trying to discipline the local community.

CARTER: I presume so.

BUCKLEY: Even though they bought the cakes?

CARTER: Well, I think the motivation for it really was to save money because—

BUCKLEY: I see.

CARTER: —as you know, the Title IV-A program, which was growing by leaps and bounds and needed some restraints, was approaching a point of about five and a half, maybe $6 billion. And Congress last September said that we're going to put a two-and-a-half-billion-dollar limit on it, and I think what Mr. Nixon and they tried to do was to pass regulations that would prevent even the expenditure of the two and a half billion dollars.

BUCKLEY: That's it. That's it. That's it.

CARTER: I believe that was motivation.

BUCKLEY: Yeah. Yeah. But Ms. Young, you wanted to make sort of a feminist point here, and I think we didn't really . . . we sort of derailed here.

YOUNG: I did want to see if you thought it was related to job discrimination since women have trouble getting into high-paying jobs, so that frequently this mother you're talking about would have a great deal of difficulty earning enough to justify her going off of welfare.

CARTER: Yes. I believe that's part of it. I've served in the legislature and now as governor and I believe a great deal of the opposition to women's rights, even the group that can recruit women to fight their battle for them, I think it's economically motivated. I think there's a great deal of opposition to seeing women paid the same wages as men for the same work . . . I don't think I've answered your question.

YOUNG: That's forgiven, yeah.

BUCKLEY: I think you won that one, didn't you? Mr. Jeffrey Stafford is instructor of government at the University of South Carolina?

JEFFREY STAFFORD: Instructor of history.

BUCKLEY: Oh, I'm sorry. Do you have a question, Mr. Stafford?

STAFFORD: Yes. Actually, either of you gentlemen can take a whack at it. It seems to me that discussions on national welfare policy almost inevitably get bogged down in details and the frittering away of certain details. Well, our president told us when he was elected that he was behind the Protestant ethic, Puritan ethic, work fair, not welfare, and he was going to propose a whole series of revisions. If the Congress would act on this, apparently, we would clarify, the problem would clear it up. Two parts to a question. First of all, do you think that President Nixon's attitude in this revision of the national welfare policy was skillfully enough motivated so that it wouldn't pass in the first place as some of his critics point out? You know, putting a floor under poverty, guaranteeing a minimum annual wage? Or do you feel that it was a specific enough proposal to work if in fact it were passed?

BUCKLEY: Well, Moynihan wrote a whole book about that.

CARTER: Yes.

BUCKLEY: But go ahead.

CARTER: I was hoping you'd answer that one. I don't—

STAFFORD: Either gentleman. That's fine.

CARTER: It's hard to say whether President Nixon was sincere when he proposed his welfare reform bill. It was done with a great deal of fanfare, as you know, and got headlines all over the world, I presume, and then he's hardly mentioned it since. I think it was discerned that it would cost maybe [an] additional $4 billion a year and would add about 17 million people onto the welfare rolls that weren't presently there, so that was the end of that as far as President Nixon was concerned. I think there's a gross example of mismanagement within the Nixon administration that prevents their discerning what are good portions of a program and which ones ought to be cast aside or supplanted by improvements. There's a twin responsibility in management. One is to have the mechanism of government as efficient and effective as possible and as open to the public and as amenable to public understanding and persuasion as possible. The other one is to legitimately discern the needs of the people and try to deliver those needs in the most efficient way, but with a compassion for their needs and with a real inclination to overcome a handicap that a person might serve. But there is no effort being made so far as I can see to discern what parts of the welfare program are working and do need to be maintained, which ones ought to be cast off or replaced, and the same thing exists in the field of manpower training where some aspects of manpower training or preparation for jobs are very efficient, and others are very inefficient, and the whole thing might be wiped down. The OEO program, which is not a popular program with the people, a poverty program, there are some aspects of it [that] have been very, very helpful in providing health services for people that never would've have had it otherwise and in providing jobs for people who never would've held jobs otherwise, but simply to terminate the entire program because there's no ability to discern what part of it ought to be maintained is a breakdown that exists now. Another very serious problem is that the local, state and federal agencies must work together. In the past, I and the other forty-nine governors have been able to guess at least what would be the attitude of the federal government by seeing what bills passed, what bills were vetoed by the president, what funds were appropriated, what funds were signed into law, and the appropriations billed by the president, then we could make our budget determinations accordingly, submit them to our state legislatures, many of whom don't meet but once every two years and proceed accordingly. Now with impoundment and with this extreme secrecy that isolates the president and his decision-making leaders from the public or from Congress, there is no way for us to predict what's going to happen in the future, and many of the states have been caught in an almost untenable position, having prepared its budget and passed it, and then have the federal funds completely changed or abolished. We have, I think, the worst interrelationship now between state governments and the federal government that we've ever seen before. There's a complete breakdown.

BUCKLEY: But isn't that the penalty for overreliance on the federal government? Now, maybe that's a requirement in Georgia, Georgia being substantially below the national average and per capita income, but I don't see why in California, for instance, if they find that there are aspects of the OEO program that they like to perpetuate, they can't go ahead and perpetuate it and do it more economically than they used to do it by sending money to the federal government, only a percentage of which flowed back.

CARTER: Well, I think, as you know, we still send money to the federal government. The federal government's financial base is not removed from the Georgia taxpayer. We pay the same rate of taxes as anybody else in the nation.

BUCKLEY: Yeah, but there's less surplus.

CARTER: Well, there's a contractual arrangement in many of these things where Congress, over a period of even generations, has evolved a working relationship between the state and local governments on one hand and the federal government on the other. We'll pay 50 percent, you pay 50 percent. Certain requirements have to be met. Well, we build our state budgets on that basis. There's been a greatly escalated income to the state governments, although we've been lucky enough in Georgia to reduce taxes recently. We still have about a 16 or 17 percent increase each year in revenue, which we spend for the people. But the shock of it, the after-the-fact divulging of a secret decision completely contrary to the expressed will of Congress, is the thing that has created difficulty with the state. It's not an overdependence on the federal government. It's a contractual relationship between the two. We are picking up part of the programs that were formally within the OEO realm. For instance, as a last act, before our own Georgia legislature adjourned about a month ago, we voted $12 million to care for the training of afflicted children to supplant $13 million that had been snatched away by the federal government at the last minute. But states don't have unlimited funds, and the problem is that with a certain increase in the gross national product, say a 100 percent, local governments—

BUCKLEY: With a gross what?

CARTER: —say with a 100 percent increase in gross national product, local governments income, based primarily on property tax, only goes up 70 percent. The state government's income based on a combination of sales tax, income tax, and so forth, on average goes up 95 percent. The federal government based entirely on the very progressive income tax goes up 130 percent. With a given increase in gross national product, which inexorably occurs, the federal government is much more able to tax the same people, you and I, me and you, to finance new kinds of programs. It's not a matter of the states and local governments not being willing to do our share. It's just an inevitable part of a nation's tax structure.

BUCKLEY: It's not inevitable. It's a psychological relationship.

CARTER: Psychological?

BUCKLEY: Psychological relationship, which you invited. There's nothing in the tax code or in the Constitution of the United States that allows the federal government to preempt the taxing power. You can do anything you want to with your state income tax, and in fact, the federal government rather obligingly allows you taxpayers to discount all state taxes from taxes paid to the federal government. But surely what you're pointing to is an attitude of dependency that has stripped the state of the kind of initiative, one of the effects of which is the recent arrogance of Mr. Nixon in playing the bigger games he's playing. It seems awfully odd to hear from a southern governor that the federal government will continue to exercise all of the initiative in deciding how much tax, because—

CARTER: Well, I didn't say that and don't say that at all. Mr. Nixon doesn't, and the federal government doesn't, have the right to take any initiative in the tax structure of the state. But the point that I'm making, obviously inadequately, is that over a period of years, the interrelationships between the federal and state and local governments have been promulgated first and then accepted as a part of our economic life, and then to have decisions made in secret at the last minute after many state legislatures have already adjourned, and said, "We are canceling this program," which was approved by Congress, vetoed by the president, and then un-overridden . . .

BUCKLEY: I agree. I agree that's the least—

CARTER: This is the kind of thing that concerns me.

BUCKLEY: False reliance, the lawyers I guess would call it, and I think you're quite right. That kind of thing oughtn't to be done, but it's also, I'll just say one more time because I'm not saying it very successfully either. It is too bad that the federal government is in a position to do that to you. In point of fact, as we all know, the state taxes have risen much, much more than federal taxes in the last decade.

CARTER: That's true.

BUCKLEY: And at count, the federal revenues are equal to 20.3 percent of the GNP, and state and local taxes are equal to almost the same.

CARTER: That's true.

BUCKLEY: But the point I want to make is that suppose there were only two states in the Union, Georgia and New York.

CARTER: Yes.

BUCKLEY: What we are really talking about is how much New York money is going to come into Georgia. This is really what it comes down to. I think it helps to view the situation as a synecdoche so that you don't have the comfort of that economic blur that makes people feel that just by turning that faucet, money is spontaneously generated and flows out into Georgia. Every time the federal government does something for Georgia, it is taking away from somebody else, isn't it? I'm not saying necessarily it shouldn't.

CARTER: Well, you know, when you say the federal government does something for Georgia, that's one thing. I think the federal government is dependent on the people of Georgia and the people of New York for financing programs of all sorts that—let's take for instance the interstate highway system. This is—

BUCKLEY: There they pay 90 percent, don't they?

CARTER: Well, the point is that everybody who buys a gallon of gas pays four cents. A New Yorker pays four cents. A Georgian pays four cents. Simply because there are more people in New York doesn't mean that the New York taxpayer is taxed heavier to pay [for] the highway system. But the point is that when we pay in our four cents into a trust fund, Congress said by law that that money should be given back to the states, partially, 90 percent. The states put up 10 percent to construct the interstate system that was designed by the Eisenhower administration, and then Mr. Nixon impounds the funds. This is what creates havoc within a state highway department—

BUCKLEY: Oh, sure.

CARTER: —which is trying to work out long-range acquisition of rights of way, design mechanisms, and so forth.

BUCKLEY: Yeah. But wouldn't you say that that is in flux in Washington now? It is by no means clear, is it, that he's going to get away with it.

CARTER: No, but—

BUCKLEY: Meanwhile, there's chaos in your state.

CARTER: But he has gotten away with it for four years and a little more. I think there've been two court test cases, both originated by Missouri, and both of them have ruled that the president did not have a right to impound funds against the expressed will of Congress. But it's a losing proposition for the whole nation. Not only are the people deprived of a right to ride on the interstate highways, but the cost of construction of those highways goes up about 9 percent, and we are delayed now, I presume, four years from constructing highways in Georgia.

BUCKLEY: Sure.

CARTER: Now we've taken action on that. Mr. Nixon withheld $47 million of money that we consider to be ours from the Highway Trust Fund. Well, our Georgia legislature, at my request, this past month allocated a sale of $60 million worth of bonds to be paid by the Georgia taxpayer to go ahead and complete the interstate system, and we figured that later on, several years in the future, when the Federal highway funds come to us, we can pay off those bonds. But here's a case of a state taking the initiative. But I don't consider the federal government to be doing the Georgia State government a favor when it sends our gasoline taxes back down to Georgia to help construct the interstate highway system.

BUCKLEY: No, but after all, we're talking about 90 percent now versus 10 percent.

CARTER: But the money was paid 100 percent by taxpayers all over the nation regardless of what state they happen to live in.

BUCKLEY: Well, you'd have to trace . . . Essentially, you've got a situation where, if the government pays 90 percent of the cost of anything to a state, it's going to encourage that state to have a spree in that department. It's very hard for the State of Georgia or the State of Mississippi not to allocate a considerable amount of its money towards the building of highways if 90 percent of the revenue for them is going to come from outside of Mississippi.

CARTER: Now the 90 percent only applies to the interstate highway system, which is approved, was approved, eight to ten years ago by the federal government. As you know, the whole interstate network was laid out and approved by the Department of Transportation in Washington. We have to build the highways between the points as prescribed eight or nine years ago when—

BUCKLEY: Well, yes, but what I'm saying is that you're going to give a priority for highways over, again say schools, precisely because there is such leverage that you have. This is an example of how hierarchies are dominated by federal dispensation, isn't it?

CARTER: Well, theoretically that's true, but both the federal highway funds and the state highway funds in Georgia come exclusively from taxes on gasoline. The people that ride on the road pay for it, and I think this is a very proper allocation of funds.

BUCKLEY: In other words, if you don't raise the money that you desire from gasoline taxes, you just don't appropriate it.

CARTER: That's exactly right.

BUCKLEY: Well, I think that's a very good system.

CARTER: Yes.

BUCKLEY: Congratulations. Mr. Skinner.

SKINNER: Mr. Buckley's comment about the welfare process whereby funds are channeled through dependents to dependents and that creates atomization of the family unit. Doesn't that seem to provide an argument for the allocation of funds on a family basis, either on the McGovern plan or on some other plan, whether it's guaranteed or not?

CARTER: Well, the way I understood Mr. McGovern's plan—I think he had several, the one that former Vice President Humphrey publicized so well in California—was that every person in the nation would be allocated, I believe, a $1,000 per year. Affluent people from New York and the poorer people from New York.

BUCKLEY: Poor people from Georgia.

CARTER: Then on that $1,000 you would pay an appropriate amount of income tax. The wealthier people would pay 60 or 70 percent income tax on that dollar and only keep thirty cents. Whereas the poorer people would keep the entire dollar. This was one approach to it. It was very similar in theory, I think, to the plan that was developed by Mr. Moynihan, Pat Moynihan, and proposed by President Nixon. It's just a guaranteed minimum annual wage. But the Congress was not willing to do it because it would have taken up a great deal of additional welfare recipients throughout the nation and would've cost a good bit more. If I remember correctly, the Nixon proposal would've cost about $4 billion more than it presently costs. I don't remember the figures on McGovern's program since it wasn't ever put to a . . .

BUCKLEY: Well, you take a thousand and multiply by 200 million people to begin with, right?

CARTER: Right.

BUCKLEY: Then you subtract whatever your back taxes and so forth.

CARTER: That's true.

BUCKLEY: As a matter of fact, I think he withdrew it, didn't he, towards the end?

CARTER: Yes. He denied that that was his real plan.

BUCKLEY: He was going to send it back to Harvard for more studies.

CARTER: I think so.

BUCKLEY: Yeah.

CARTER: He said originally, really, to be fair to him, that he had three or four plans, and that particular plan was just one they were considering, but it was the one that was most obviously disadvantageous politically, and it was one that Hubert Humphrey publicized quite well.

BUCKLEY: Thank you very much to our Governor Carter. Thank you, ladies and gentlemen, with the panel. Ladies and gentlemen.

"JIMMY, WE HARDLY KNOW Y'ALL"

INTERVIEW BY ROBERT SCHEER
PLAYBOY
NOVEMBER 1976

ROBERT SCHEER: After nearly two years on the campaign trail, don't you feel a little numbed by the routine—for instance having to give the same speech over and over?

JIMMY CARTER: Sometimes. Once, when I was campaigning in the Florida primary, I made twelve speeches in one day. It was the worst day I ever had. But I generally have tried to change the order of the speech and emphasize different things. Sometimes I abbreviate and sometimes I elaborate. Of twenty different parts in a speech, I might take seven or eight and change them around. It depends on the audience—Black people, Jewish people, Chicanos—and that gives me the ability to make speeches that aren't boring to myself.

SCHEER: Every politician probably emphasizes different things to different audiences, but in your case, there's been a common criticism that you seem to have several faces, that you try to be all things to all people. How do you respond to that?

CARTER: I can't make myself believe these are contrivances and subterfuges I've adopted to get votes. It may be, and I can't get myself to admit it, but what I want to do is to let people know how I stand on the issues as honestly as I can.

SCHEER: If you feel you've been fully honest, why has the charge persisted that you're "fuzzy" on the issues?

CARTER: It started during the primaries when most of my opponents were members of Congress. When any question on an issue came up, they would say, "I'm for the Kennedy-Corman bill on health care, period, no matter what's in it." If the question was on unemployment, they would say, "I'm for the Humphrey-Hawkins bill, no matter what's in it." But those bills were constantly being amended! I'm just not able to do that. I have to understand what I'm talking about, and simplistic answers identifying my position with such and such a House bill are something I can't put forward. That's one reason I've been seen as fuzzy. Another is that I'm not an ideologue and my positions are not predictable. Without any criticism of McGovern, if the question had ever come up on abortion, you could pretty well anticipate what he was going to say. If it were amnesty, you could predict what McGovern was going to say about that. But I've tried to analyze each question individually; I've taken positions that to me are fair and rational, and sometimes my answers are complicated.

The third reason is that I wasn't a very vulnerable opponent for those who ran against me. Fuzziness was the only issue Congressman Udall, Senator Church—and others that are hard to remember now—could adopt in their campaigns against me. I think the drumming of that factor into the consciousness of the American voter obviously had some impact.

SCHEER: Still, not everybody's sure whether you're a conservative in liberal clothing or vice versa. FDR, for instance, turned out to be something of a surprise to people who'd voted for him, because he hadn't seemed as progressive before he was elected as he turned out to be. Could you be a surprise that way?

CARTER: I don't believe that's going to be the case. If you analyze the Democratic Party platform, you'll see that it's a very progressive, very liberal, very socially motivated platform. What sometimes surprises people is that I carry out my promises. People ask how a peanut farmer from the South who believes in balanced budgets and tough management of government can possibly give the country tax and welfare reform or a national health program or insist on equal rights for Blacks and women. Well, I'm going to do those things. I've promised them during the campaign, so I don't think there will be many people disappointed—or surprised—when I carry out those commitments as president.

SCHEER: But isn't it true that you turned out to be more liberal as governor of Georgia than people who voted for you had any reason to suspect?

CARTER: I don't really think so. No, *The Atlanta Constitution*, which was the source of all information about me, categorized me during the gubernatorial campaign as an ignorant, racist, ultraconservative, rednecked South Georgia peanut farmer. Its candidate, Carl Sanders, the former governor, was characterized as an enlightened, progressive, well-educated, urbane, forceful, competent public official. I never agreed with the categorization that was made of me during the campaign. I was the same person before and after I became governor. I remember keeping a checklist and every time I made a promise during the campaign, I wrote it down in a notebook. I believe I carried out every promise I made. I told several people during the campaign that one of the phrases I was going to use in my inaugural speech was that the time for racial discrimination was over. I wrote and made that speech.

The ultraconservatives in Georgia—who aren't supporting me now, by the way—voted for me because of their animosity toward Carl Sanders. I was the alternative to him. They never asked me, "Are you a racist or have you been a member of the Ku Klux Klan?" because they knew I wasn't and hadn't been. And yet, despite predictions early this year by *The Atlanta Constitution* that I couldn't get a majority of the primary vote in Georgia against Wallace, I received about 85 percent of the votes. So, I don't think the Georgia people have the feeling I betrayed them.

SCHEER: Considering what you've just said about *The Atlanta Constitution*, how do you feel about the media in general and about the job they do in covering the election issues?

CARTER: There's still a tendency on the part of some members of the press to treat the South, you know, as a suspect nation. There are a few who think that I am a southern governor, I must be a secret racist or there's something in a closet somewhere that's going to be revealed to show my true colors. There's been a constant probing back ten, twelve years in my background, even as early as the first primaries. Nobody probed like that into the background of Udall or

Bayh or other people. But I don't object to it particularly, I just recognize it.

(The answer was broken off and at a later session, Carter returned to the question of the press and its coverage of issues. This time he was tired, his head sunk far back into his airplane seat. The exchange occurred during one of the late primaries.)

CARTER: Issues? The local media are interested, all right, but the national news media have absolutely no interest in issues at all. Sometimes we freeze out the national media so we can open up press conferences to local people. At least we get questions from them—on timber management, on health care, on education. But the traveling press have zero interest in any issue unless it's a matter of making a mistake. What they're looking for is a forty-seven-second argument between me and another candidate or something like that. There's nobody in the back of this plane who would ask an issue question unless he thought he could trick me into some crazy statement.

SCHEER: One crazy statement you were supposed to have made was reported by Robert Shrum after he quit as your speechwriter earlier this year. He said he'd been in conversations with you when you made some slighting references to Jewish voters. What's your version of what happened?

CARTER: Shrum dreamed up eight or ten conversations that never took place and nobody in the press ever asked me if they had occurred. The press just assumed that they had. I never talked to Shrum in private except for maybe a couple of minutes. If he had told the truth, if I had said all the things he claimed I had said, I wouldn't vote for *myself*.

When a poll came out early in the primaries that said I had a small proportion of the Jewish vote, I said, "Well, this is really a disappointment to me—we've worked so hard with the Jewish voters. But my pro-Israel stand won't change, even if I don't get a single Jewish vote; I guess we'll have to depend on non-Jews to put me in office." But Shrum treated it as if it were some kind of racist disavowal of Jews. Well, that's a kind of sleazy twisting of a conversation.

SCHEER: While we're on the subject of the press, how do you feel about an issue that concerns the press itself—the right of journalists to keep their sources secret?

CARTER: I would do everything I could to protect the secrecy of sources for the news media.

SCHEER: Both the press *and* the public seem to have made an issue out of your Baptist beliefs. Why do you think this has happened?

CARTER: I'm not unique. There are a lot of people in this country who have the same religious faith. It's not a mysterious or mythical or magical thing. But for those who don't know the feeling of someone who believes in Christ, who is aware of the presence of God, there is, I presume, a quizzical attitude toward it. But it's always been something I've discussed very frankly throughout my adult life.

SCHEER: We heard that you pray twenty-five times a day. Is it true?

CARTER: I've never counted. I've forgotten who asked me that, but I'd say that on an eventful day, you know, it's something like that.

SCHEER: When you say an eventful day, do you mean you pray as a kind of pause to control your blood pressure and relax?

CARTER: Well, yes. If something happens to me that is a little disconcerting, if I feel a trepidation, if a thought comes into my head of animosity or hatred toward someone, then I just kind of say a brief silent prayer. I don't ask for myself but just to let me understand what another's feelings might be. Going through a crowd, quite often people bring me a problem, and I pray that their needs might be met. A lot of times, I'll be in the back seat of a car and not know what kind of audience I'm going to face. I don't mean I'm terror-stricken, just that I don't know what to expect next. I'll pray then, but it's not something that's conscious or formal. It's just a part of my life.

SCHEER: One reason some people might be quizzical is that you have a sister, Ruth, who is a faith healer. The association of politics with faith healing is an idea many find disconcerting.

CARTER: I don't even know what political ideas that Ruth has had, and for people to suggest I'm under the hold of a sister—or any other person—is a complete distortion of fact.

I don't have any idea whether Ruth has supported Democrats or not, whereas the political views of my other sister, Gloria, are remarkably harmonious with mine.

SCHEER: So, you're closer to Gloria, who has described herself as a McGovern Democrat and rides motorcycles as a hobby?

CARTER: I like them both. But in the past twenty or twenty-five years, I've been much closer to Gloria, because she lives next door to me, and Ruth lives in North Carolina. We hardly saw Ruth more than once a year at family get-togethers. What political attitudes Ruth has had, I have not the slightest idea. But my mother and Gloria and I have been very compatible. We supported Lyndon Johnson openly during the 1964 campaign and my mother worked at the Johnson county headquarters, which was courageous, not an easy thing to do politically. She would come out of the Johnson headquarters and find her car smeared with soap and the antenna tied in a knot and ugly messages left on the front seat. When my young boys went to school, they were beaten. So, my mother and Gloria and I, along with my Rosalynn, have had the same attitudes even when we were in a minority in Plains. But Ruth lives in a different world in North Carolina.

SCHEER: Granting that you're not as close to your religious sister as is assumed, we still wonder how your religious beliefs would translate into political action. For instance, would you appoint judges who would be harsh or lenient towards victimless crimes—offenses such as drug use, adultery, sodomy and homosexuality?

CARTER: Committing adultery, according to the Bible— which I believe in—is a sin. For us to hate one another, for us to have sexual intercourse outside marriage, for us to engage in homosexual activities, for us to steal, for us to lie—all these are sins. But Jesus teaches us not to judge other people. We don't assume the role of judge and say to another human being, "You're condemned because you commit sins." All Christians, all of us, acknowledge that we are sinful, and the judgment comes from God, not from another human being.

As governor of Georgia, I tried to shift the emphasis of law enforcement away from victimless crimes. We lessened the penalties on the use of marijuana. We removed alcoholism as a crime, and so forth. Victimless crimes, in my opinion, should have a very low priority in terms of enforcing the laws on the books. But as to appointing judges, that would not be the basis on which I'd appoint them. I would choose people who were competent, whose judgment and integrity were sound. I think it would be inappropriate to ask them how they were going to rule on a particular question before I appointed them.

SCHEER: What *about* those laws on the books that govern personal behavior? Should they be enforced?

CARTER: Almost every state in the Union has laws against adultery and many of them have laws against homosexuality and sodomy. But they're often considered by police officers as not worthy of enforcing to the extent of disturbing consenting adults or breaking into a person's private home.

SCHEER: But, of course, that gives the police a lot of leeway to enforce them selectively. Do you think such laws should be on the books at all?

CARTER: That's a judgment for the individual states to make. I think the laws are on the books quite often because of their relationship to the Bible. Early in the nation's development, the Judeo-Christian moral standards were accepted as a basis for civil law. But I don't think it hurts to have this kind of standard maintained as a goal. I also think it's an area that's been interpreted by the Supreme Court as one that can rightfully be retained by the individual states.

SCHEER: Do you think liberalization of the laws over the past decade by factors as diverse as the pill and *Playboy*—an effect some people would term permissiveness—has been a harmful development?

CARTER: Liberalization of some of the laws has been good. You can't legislate morality. We tried to outlaw consumption of alcoholic beverages. We found that violation of the law led to bigger crimes and bred disrespect for the law.

SCHEER: We're confused. You say morality can't be legislated, yet you support certain laws because they preserve old moral standards. How do you reconcile the two positions?

CARTER: I believe people should honor civil laws. If there is a conflict between God's law and civil law, we should honor God's law. But we should be willing to accept civil punishment. Most of Christ's original followers were killed because of their belief in Christ; they violated the civil law in following God's law. Reinhold Niebuhr, a theologian who has dealt with this problem at length, says that the framework of law is a balancing of forces in a society; the law itself tends to alleviate tensions brought about by these forces. But the laws on the books are not a measure of this balance nearly as much as the degree to which the laws are enforced. So, when a law is anachronistic and is carried over from a previous age, it's just not observed.

SCHEER: What we're getting at is how much you'd tolerate behavior that your religion considers wrong. For instance, in San Francisco, you said you considered homosexuality a sin. What does that mean in political terms?

CARTER: The issue of homosexuality always makes me nervous. It's obviously one of the major issues in San Francisco. I don't have any, you know, personal knowledge about homosexuality and I guess being a Baptist, that would contribute to a sense of being uneasy.

SCHEER: Does it make you uneasy to discuss it simply as a political question?

CARTER: No, it's more complicated than that. It's political, it's moral and it's strange territory for me. At home in Plains, we've had homosexuals in our community, our church. There's never been any sort of discrimination—some embarrassment but no animosity, no harassment. But to inject it into a public discussion on politics and how it conflicts with morality is a new experience for me. I've thought about it a lot, but I don't see how to handle it differently from the way I look on other sexual acts outside of marriage.

SCHEER: We'd like to ask you a blunt question: Isn't it just these views about what's "sinful" and what's "immoral" that contribute to the feeling that you might get a call from God, or get inspired and push the wrong button? More realistically, wouldn't we expect a puritanical tone to be set in the White House if you were elected?

CARTER: Harry Truman was a Baptist. Some people get very abusive about the Baptist faith. If people want to know about it, they can read the New Testament. The main thing is that we don't think we're better than anyone else. We are taught not to judge other people. But as to some of the behavior you've mentioned, I can't change the teachings of Christ. I can't change the teachings of Christ! I believe in them, and a lot of people in this country do as well. Jews believe in the Bible. They have the same commandments.

SCHEER: Then you as president, in appointing Supreme Court justices—

CARTER: I think we've pursued this conversation long enough—if you have another question . . . Look, I'll try to express my views. It's not a matter of condemnation, it's not a matter of persecution. I've been a governor for four years. Anybody can come and look at my record. I didn't run around breaking down people's doors to see if they were fornicating. This is something that's ridiculous.

SCHEER: We know you didn't, but we're being persistent because of this matter of self-righteousness, because of the moral certainty of so many of your statements. People wonder if Jimmy Carter ever is unsure. Has he ever been wrong, has he ever had a failure of moral nerve?

CARTER: Well, there are a lot of things I could have done differently had I known during my early life what I now know. I would certainly have spoken out more clearly and loudly on the civil rights issue. I would have demanded that our nation never get involved initially in the Vietnam War. I would have told the country in 1972 that Watergate was a much more horrible crime than we thought at the time. It's easy to say in hindsight what you would have done if you had had information you now have.

SCHEER: We were asking not so much about hindsight as about being fallible. Aren't there any examples of things you did that weren't absolutely right?

CARTER: I don't mind repeating myself. There are a lot of those in my life. Not speaking out for the cessation of the war in Vietnam. The fact that I didn't crusade at a very early stage for civil rights in the South, for the one-man, one-vote ruling. It might be that now I should drop my campaign for president and start a crusade for Black-majority rule in South Africa or Rhodesia. It might be that later on, we'll discover there were opportunities in our lives to do wonderful things and we didn't take advantage of them.

The fact that in 1954 I sat back and required the Warren Court to make this ruling without having crusaded myself—that was obviously a mistake on my part. But these are things you have to judge under the circumstances that prevailed when the decisions were being made. Back then, the Congress, the president, the newspaper editors, the civil libertarians all said that separate-but-equal facilities were adequate. These are opportunities overlooked, or maybe they could be characterized as absence of courage.

SCHEER: Since you seem to be saying you'd have done the right thing if you'd known what you know now, is it realistic to conclude that a person running for the highest office in the land can't *admit* many mistakes or moments of self-doubt?

CARTER: I think that's a human circumstance. But if there are issues [that] I'm avoiding because of a lack of courage, either I don't recognize them, or I can't make myself recognize them.

SCHEER: You mentioned Vietnam. Do you feel you spoke out at an early enough stage against the war?

CARTER: No. I did not. I never spoke out publicly about withdrawing completely from Vietnam until March of 1971.

SCHEER: Why?

CARTER: It was the first time anybody had asked me about it. I was a farmer before then and wasn't asked about the war until I took office. There was a general feeling in this country that we ought not to be in Vietnam to start with. The American people were tremendously misled about the immediate prospects for victory, about the level of our involvement, about the relative cost in American lives. If I had known in the sixties what I knew in the early seventies, I think I would have spoken out more strongly. I was not in public office. When I took office as governor in 1970, I began to speak out about complete withdrawal. It was late compared with what many others had done, but I think it's accurate to say that Congress and the people—with the exception of very small numbers of people—shared the belief that we were protecting our democratic allies.

SCHEER: Even without holding office, you must have had some feelings about the war. When do you recall first feeling it was wrong?

CARTER: There was an accepted feeling by me and everybody else that we ought not to be there, that we should never have gotten involved, we ought to get out.

SCHEER: You felt that way all through the sixties?

CARTER: Yeah, that's right, and I might hasten to say that it was the same feeling expressed by Senators Russell and Talmadge—very conservative southern political figures. They thought it was a serious mistake to be in Vietnam.

SCHEER: Your son Jack fought in that war. Did you have any qualms about it at the time?

CARTER: Well, yes, I had problems about my son fighting in the war, period. But I never make my sons' decisions for them. Jack went to war feeling it was foolish, a waste of time, much more deeply than I did. He also felt it would have been grossly unfair for him not to go when other, poorer kids had to.

SCHEER: You were in favor of allocating funds for the South Vietnamese in 1975 as the war was coming to a close, weren't you?

CARTER: That was when we were getting ready to evacuate our troops. The purpose of the money was to get our people out and maintain harmony between us and our Vietnamese allies, who had fought with us for twenty-five years. And I said yes, I would do that. But it was not a permanent thing, not to continue the war but to let us get our troops out in an orderly fashion.

SCHEER: How do you respond to the argument that it was the Democrats, not the Republicans, who got us into the Vietnam War?

CARTER: I think it started originally, maybe, with Eisenhower, then Kennedy, Johnson and then Nixon. It's not a partisan matter. I think Eisenhower probably first got us in there thinking since France had failed, our country might slip in there and succeed. Kennedy thought he could escalate involvement by going beyond the mere advisory role. I guess if there was one president who made the most determined effort, conceivably, to end the war by massive force, it was certainly Johnson. And Nixon went into Cambodia and bombed it, and so forth. It's not partisan—it's just a matter that evolved as a habit over several administrations. There was a governmental consciousness to deal in secrecy, to exclude the American people, to mislead them with false statements and sometimes outright lies. Had the American people been told the facts from the beginning by Eisenhower, Kennedy, McNamara, Johnson, Kissinger and Nixon, I think there would have been different decisions made in our government.

SCHEER: At the Democratic Convention, you praised Johnson as a president who had vastly extended human rights. Were you simply omitting any mention of Vietnam?

CARTER: It was obviously the factor that destroyed his political career and damaged his whole life. But as far as what, as what I said at the convention, there hasn't been another president in our history—with the possible exception of Abraham Lincoln—who did so much to advance the cause of human rights.

SCHEER: Except for the human rights of the Vietnamese and the Americans who fought there.

CARTER: Well, I really believe that Johnson's motives were good. I think he tried to end the war even while the fighting was going on, and he was speaking about massive rehabilitation efforts, financed by our government, to help people. I don't think he ever had any desire for permanent entrenchment of our forces in Vietnam. I think he had a mistaken notion that he was defending democracy and that what he was doing was compatible with the desires of the South Vietnamese.

SCHEER: Then what about the administration that ended the war? Don't you have to give credit to Kissinger, the secretary of a Republican president, for ending a war that a Democratic president escalated?

CARTER: I think the statistics show that more bombs were dropped in Vietnam and Cambodia under Nixon and Kissinger than under Johnson. Both administrations were at fault, but I don't think the end came about as a result of Kissinger's superior diplomacy. It was the result of several factors that built up in an inexorable way: the demonstrated strength of the Viet Cong, the tremendous pressure to withdraw that came from the American people, and an aroused Congress. I think Nixon and Kissinger did the proper thing in starting a phased withdrawal, but I don't consider that to be a notable diplomatic achievement by Kissinger. As we've now learned, he promised the Vietnamese things that cannot be delivered—reparations, payments, economic advantages, and so forth. Getting out of Vietnam was very good, but whether Kissinger deserved substantial diplomatic credit for it is something I doubt.

SCHEER: You've said you'd pardon men who refused military service because of the Vietnam War but not necessarily those who deserted while they were in the armed forces. Is that right?

CARTER: That's right. I would not include them. Deserters ought to be handled on a separate-case basis. There's a difference to me. I was in the Navy for a long time. Somebody who goes into the military joins a kind of mutual partnership arrangement, you know what I mean? Your life depends on other people, their lives depend on you. So, I don't intend to pardon the deserters. As far as the other categories of war resisters go, to me, the ones who stayed in this country and let their opposition to the war be known publicly are more heroic than those who went and hid in Sweden. But I'm not capable of judging motives, so I'm just going to declare a blanket pardon.

SCHEER: When?

CARTER: The first week I'm in office.

SCHEER: You've avoided the word "amnesty" and chosen to use the word "pardon," but there doesn't seem to be much difference between the two in the dictionary. Could it be because "amnesty" is more emotionally charged and "pardon" a word more people will accept?

CARTER: You know I can't deny that. But my reason for distinguishing between the two is that I think that all of those poor, and often Black, young men who went to Vietnam are more worthy of recognition than those who defected, and the word "pardon" includes those who simply avoided the war completely. But I just want to bring the defectors back to this country without punishment and, in doing so, I would like to have the support of the American people. I haven't been able to devise for private or public presentation a better way to do it.

SCHEER: Earlier this year there was a report that as Governor of Georgia, you had issued a resolution that seemed to support William Calley after his trial for the My Lai massacre and that you referred to him as a scapegoat. Was that a misreading of your position?

CARTER: Yes. There was no reason for me to mislead anybody on the Calley thing. I thought when I first read about him that Calley was a murderer. He was tried in Georgia and found to be a murderer. I said two things: one, that Calley was not typical of our American servicemen and, two, that he was a scapegoat because his superiors should have been tried, too. The resolution I made as governor didn't have anything to do with Calley. The purpose of it, calling for solidarity with our boys in Vietnam, was to distinguish American servicemen fighting an unpopular war. They weren't murderers, but they were equated, unfortunately, with a murderer in people's minds.

SCHEER: In preparing for this interview, we spoke with your mother, your son Chip and your sister Gloria. We asked them what single action would most disappoint them in a Carter presidency. They all replied that it would be if you ever sent troops to intervene in a foreign war. In fact, Miss Lillian said she would picket the White House.

CARTER: They share my views completely.

SCHEER: What about more limited military action? Would you have handled the Mayagüez incident the same way President Ford did?

CARTER: Let me assess that in retrospect. It's obvious we didn't have adequate intelligence; we attacked an island when the Mayagüez crew was no longer there. There was a desire, I think, on the part of President Ford to extract maximum publicity from our effort, so that, about twenty-three minutes after our crew was released, we went ahead and bombed the island airport. I hope I would have been capable of getting adequate intelligence, surrounded the island more quickly and isolated the crew so we wouldn't have had to attack the airport after the crew was released. These are some of the differences in the way I would have done it.

SCHEER: So, it's a matter of degree; you would have intervened militarily, too.

CARTER: I would have done everything necessary to keep the crew from being taken to the mainland, yes.

SCHEER: Then would you summarize your position on foreign intervention?

CARTER: I would never intervene for the purpose of overthrowing a government. If enough were at stake for our national interest, I would use prestige, legitimate diplomatic leverage, trade mechanisms. But it would be the sort of effort that would not be embarrassing to this nation if revealed completely. I don't ever want to do anything as president that would be a contravention of the moral and ethical standards that I would exemplify in my own life as an individual or that would violate the principles or character of the American people.

SCHEER: Do you feel it's a fair criticism that you seem to be going back to some familiar faces—such as Paul Warnke and Cyrus Vance—for foreign-policy advice? Isn't there a danger of history repeating itself when you seek out those who were involved in our Vietnam decisions?

CARTER: I haven't heard that criticism. If you're raising it, then I respond to the new critic. These people contribute to foreign-affairs journals, they individually explore different concepts of foreign policy. I have fifteen or twenty people who work with me very closely on foreign affairs. Their views are quite divergent. The fact that they may or may not have been involved in foreign-policy decisions in the past is certainly no detriment to their ability to help me now.

SCHEER: In some respects, your foreign policy seems similar to that established by Kissinger, Nixon and Ford. In fact, Kissinger stated that he didn't think your differences were substantial. How, precisely, does your view differ from theirs?

CARTER: As I've said in my speeches, I feel the policy of détente has given up too much to the Russians and gotten too little in return. I also feel Kissinger has equated his own popularity with the so-called advantages of détente. As I've traveled and spoken with world leaders—Helmut Schmidt of West Germany, Yitzhak Rabin of Israel, various leaders in Japan—I've discerned a deep concern on their part that the United States has abandoned a long-standing principle: to consult mutually, to share responsibility for problems. This has been a damaging thing. In addition, I believe we should have stronger bilateral relations with developing nations.

SCHEER: What do you mean when you say we've given up too much to the Russians?

CARTER: One example I've mentioned often is the Helsinki Agreement. I never saw any reason we should be involved in the Helsinki meetings at all. We added the statue of our presence and signature to an agreement that, in effect, ratified the takeover of Eastern Europe by the Soviet Union. We got very little, if anything, in return. The Russians promised they would honor democratic principles and permit the free movement of their citizens, including those who want to emigrate. The Soviet Union has not lived up to those promises and Mr. Brezhnev was able to celebrate the major achievement of his diplomatic life.

SCHEER: Are you charging that Kissinger was too soft on the Russians?

CARTER: Kissinger has been in the position of being almost uniquely a spokesman for our nation. I think that is a legitimate role and proper responsibility of the president himself. Kissinger has had a kind of Lone Ranger, secret foreign-policy attitude, which almost ensures that there cannot be adequate consultation with our allies; there cannot be a long-range commitment to unchanging principles; there cannot be a coherent evolution on foreign policy; there cannot be a bipartisan approach with support and advice from Congress. That is what I would avoid as president and is one of the major defects in the Nixon-Ford foreign policy as expressed by Kissinger.

SCHEER: Say, do you always do your own sewing?

(This portion of the interview also took place aboard a plane. As he answered the interviewer's questions, Carter had been sewing a rip in his jacket with a needle and thread he carried with him.)

CARTER: Uh-huh. [*He bit off the thread with his teeth.*]

SCHEER: Anyway, you said earlier that your foreign policy would exemplify your moral and ethical standards. Isn't there as much danger in overly moralistic policy as in the kind that is too pragmatic?

CARTER: I've said I don't think we should intervene militarily, but I see no reason not to express our approval, at least verbally, with those nations that develop democratically.

When Kissinger says, as he did recently in a speech, that Brazil is the sort of government that is most compatible with ours—well, that's the kind of thing we want to change. Brazil is not a democratic government; it's a military dictatorship. In many instances, it's highly repressive to political prisoners. Our government should justify the character and moral principles of the American people, and our foreign policy should not short-circuit that for temporary advantage. I think in every instance we've done that, it's been counterproductive. When the CIA undertakes covert activities that might be justified if they were peaceful, we always suffer when they're revealed—it always seems as if we're trying to tell other people how to act. When Kissinger and Ford warned Italy she would be excluded from NATO if the Communists assumed power, that was the best way to make sure Communists were elected. The Italian voters resent it. A proper posture for our country in this sort of situation is to show, through demonstration, that our own government works properly, that democracy is advantageous, and let the Italian people make their own decisions.

SCHEER: And what if the Communists in Italy had been elected in greater numbers than they were? What if they had actually become a key part of the Italian government?

CARTER: I think it would be a mechanism for subversion of the strength of NATO and the cohesiveness that ought to bind European countries together. The proper posture was the one taken by Helmut Schmidt, who said that German aid to Italy would be endangered.

SCHEER: Don't you think that constitutes a form of intervention in the democratic processes of another nation?

CARTER: No, I don't. I think that when the democratic nations of the world express themselves frankly and forcefully and openly, that's a proper exertion of influence. We did the same thing in Portugal. Instead of going in through surreptitious means and trying to overthrow the government when it looked like the minority Communist Party was going to assume power, the NATO countries as a group made it clear to Portugal what it would lose in the way of friendship, trade opportunities, and so forth. And the Portuguese people, recognizing the possibility, decided that the Communists should not lead their government. Well, that was legitimate exertion of influence, in my opinion. It was done openly, and it was a mere statement of fact.

SCHEER: You used the word "subversion" referring to communism. Hasn't the world changed since we used to throw words like that around? Aren't the West European communist parties more independent of Moscow and more willing to respect democracy?

CARTER: Yes, the world's changed. In my speeches, I've made it clear that as far as Communist leaders in such countries as Italy, France and Portugal are concerned, I would not want to close the doors of communication, consultation and friendship to them. That would be an almost automatic forcing of the Communist leaders into the Soviet sphere of influence. I also think we should keep open our opportunities for the East European nations—even those that are completely Communist—to trade with us, understand us, have tourist exchange and give them an option from complete domination by the Soviet Union.

But again, I don't think you could expect West Germany to lend Poland $2 billion—which was the figure in the case of Italy—when Poland is part of the Soviet government's satellite and supportive-nation group. So, I think the best way to minimize totalitarian influence within the governments of Europe is to make sure the democratic forces perform properly. The major shift toward the Communists in Italy was in the local elections when the Christian Democrats destroyed their reputation by graft and corruption. If we can make our own government work, if we can avoid future Watergates and avoid the activities of the CIA that have been revealed, if we can minimize joblessness and inflation, this will be a good way to lessen the inclination of people in other countries to turn away from our form of government.

SCHEER: What about Chile? Would you agree that that was a case of the United States, through the CIA, intervening improperly?

CARTER: Yes. There's no doubt about it. Sure.

SCHEER: And you would stop that sort of thing?

CARTER: Absolutely. Yes, sir.

SCHEER: What about economic sanctions? Do you feel we should have punished the Allende government the way we did?

CARTER: That's a complicated question because we don't know what caused the fall of the Allende government, the murder of perhaps thousands of people, the incarceration of many others. I don't have any facts as to how deeply involved we were, but my impression is that we were involved quite deeply. As I said, I wouldn't have done that if I were president. But as to whether or not we ought to have an option on the terms of our loans, repayment schedules, interest charges, the kinds of materials we sell to them—those are options I would retain depending upon the compatibility of a foreign government with our own.

SCHEER: To what do you attribute all those deceptions and secret maneuverings through the years? Why were they allowed to happen?

CARTER: It was a matter of people's just saying, well, that's politics; we don't have a right to know what our government is doing; secrecy is OK; accepting gifts is OK; excluding the American people is OK. These are the kinds of things I want to change.

SCHEER: It sounds as if you're saying Americans accepted indecency and lies in their government all too easily. Doesn't that make your constant campaign theme, invoking the decency and honesty of the American people, somewhat naïve and ingenuous?

CARTER: I say that the American people are basically decent and honest and want a truthful government. Obviously, I know there are people in this country, out of 214 million, who are murderers. There are people, maybe who don't want a decent government. Maybe there are people who prefer lies to truth. But I don't think it's simplistic to say that our government hasn't measured up to the ethical and moral standards of the people of this country. We've had better governments in the past and I think our people, as I've said many times, are just as strong, courageous and intelligent as they were two hundred years ago. I think we still have the same inner strength they had then.

SCHEER: Even though a lot of people support that feeling, many others think it makes you sound like an evangelist. And that makes it all the more confusing when they read about your hanging out with people so different from you in lifestyle and beliefs. Your publicized friendship with journalist Hunter Thompson, who makes no secret of his affinity for drugs and other craziness, is a good example.

CARTER: Well, in the first place, I'm a human being. I'm not a packaged article that you can put in a little box and say, "Here's a Southern Baptist, an ignorant Georgia peanut farmer who doesn't have the right to enjoy music, who has no flexibility in his mind, who can't understand the sensitivities of an interpersonal relationship. He's gotta be predictable. He's gotta be for Calley and for the war. He's gotta be a liar. He's gotta be a racist." You know, that's the sort of stereotype people tend to assume, and I hope it doesn't apply to me. And

I don't see any mystery about having a friendship with Hunter Thompson. I guess it's something that's part of my character and it becomes a curiosity for those who see some mystery about someone of my background being elected president. I'm just a human being like everybody else. I have different interests, different understandings of the world around me, different relationships with different kinds of people. I have a broad range of friends: sometimes very serious, sometimes very formal, sometimes lighthearted, sometimes intense, sometimes casual.

SCHEER: So, when you find yourself at a rock concert or in some other situation that seems at odds with your rural, religious background, you never feel a sense of estrangement?

CARTER: None. No, I feel at home with 'em.

SCHEER: How did you get to feel this way without going through culture shock?

CARTER: I have three sons who now range from twenty-three to twenty-nine, and the oldest of them were very influenced by Bob Dylan in their attitudes with civil rights, criminal justice and the Vietnam War. This was about the period of time I was entering politics. I've been fairly close to my sons and their taste in music influenced my taste, and I was able to see the impact of Bob Dylan's attitudes on young people. And I was both gratified by and involved emotionally in those changes of attitudes.

Later, when I became governor, I was acquainted with some of the people at Capricorn Records in Macon—Otis Redding and others. It was they who began to meld the white and black music industries, and that was quite a sociological change for our region. So, as I began to travel around Georgia, I made contact a few days every month or two with Capricorn Records, just to stay in touch with people in the state, and got to know all the Allman Brothers, Dickey Betts and others. Later on, I met Charlie Daniels and the Marshall Tucker Band.

Then I decided to run for president. I didn't have any money and didn't have any political base, so I had to depend substantially on the friends I already had. One of my potential sources for fundraising and for recruiting young volunteers was the group of recording stars I already knew. So, we began to have concerts and I got to know them even better.

Of course, I've also been close to the country-music folks in Georgia, as well as the Atlanta Symphony Orchestra. The first large contribution I got—$1,000—was from Robert Shaw, the music director of the orchestra. We've been all over at the Grand Ole Opry a few times and gotten to know people like Chubby Jackson and Tom T. Hall.

SCHEER: There's been a lot of publicity about your relationship with Dylan, whom you quoted in your acceptance speech at the Democratic Convention. How did that come about?

CARTER: A number of years ago, my second son, Chip, who was working full-time in our farming business, took a week off during Christmas. He and a couple of his friends drove all the way to New York just to see Bob Dylan. There had been a heavy snowstorm and the boys had to park several miles from Dylan's home. It was after Dylan was injured when he was in seclusion. Apparently, Dylan came to the door with two of his kids and shook hands with Chip. By the time Chip got to the nearest phone a couple of miles away and called us at home, he was nearly incoherent. Rosalynn couldn't understand what Chip was talking about, so she screamed, "Jimmy, come here quick! Something's happened to Chip!"

We finally deciphered that he had shaken Dylan's hand, was just, you know, very carried away with it. So, when I read Dylan was going on tour again, I wrote him a little personal note and asked him to come visit me at the governor's mansion. I think he checked with Phil Walden of Capricorn Records and Bill Graham to find out what kind of guy is this, and he was assured I didn't want to use him, I was just interested in his music.

The night he came, we had a chance to talk about his music and about changing times and pent-up emotion in young people. He said he didn't have any inclination to change the world, that he wasn't crusading and that his personal feelings were apparently compatible with the yearnings of an entire generation. We also discussed Israel, which he had a strong interest in. But that's my only contact with Bob Dylan, that night.

SCHEER: That brings us back to the reason so many people find it hard to get a handle on you: on the one hand, your association with youth culture, civil rights and other liberal movements; and on the other, your apparent conservatism on many issues. Would you care to put it in a nutshell for us?

CARTER: I'll try. On human rights, civil rights, environmental quality, I consider myself to be very liberal. On the management of government, on openness of government, on strengthening individual liberties and local levels of government, I consider myself a conservative. And I don't see that the two attitudes are incompatible.

SCHEER: Then let's explore a few more issues. Not everyone is sure, for instance, what you mean by your call for tax reform. Does it mean that the burden will shift to corporations and upper-income groups and away from the middle- and lower-income groups, or are you talking merely about a simplified tax code?

CARTER: It would involve both. One change I'm calling for is simplification, and the other involves shifting the income tax burden away from the lower-income families. But what I'm really talking about is total, comprehensive tax reform for the first time since the income tax was approved back in 1913, I think it was. It's not possible to give you a definitive statement on tax reform anytime soon. It's going to take at least a year before we can come up with a new tax structure. But there are some general provisions that would be instituted that aren't there now. The income-tax code, which now comprises forty thousand pages, will be greatly simplified. Income should be taxed only once. We should have a true progressive income tax, so that the higher the income, the higher the percentage of taxation. I see no reason why capital gains should be taxed at half the rate of income from manual labor. I would be committed to a great reduction in tax incentives, loopholes or whatever you want to call them, which are used as mechanisms to solve transient economic problems; they ought to be on a basis of annual appropriation or a time limit, rather than be built into the tax structure. In any case, there are five or six things that would be dramatic departures from what we presently have, and they should tell you what side of the issue I stand on.

SCHEER: Would one of those be increasing taxes for corporations, especially the overseas and domestic profits of multinational corporations?

CARTER: No, I don't think so. Obviously, there have been provisions written into the law that favor certain corporations, including those that have overseas investments; I would remove those incentives. Tax laws also benefit those who have the best lobbying efforts, those who have the most influence in Washington, and the larger the corporations are, on the average, the similar proportion they pay in taxes. Small businesses quite often pay the flat maximum rate, 48 percent, while some larger corporations pay as little as 5 or 6 percent. That ought to be changed. But as far as increasing overall corporate taxes above the 50 percent level, I wouldn't favor that. We also have the circumstance of multinational corporations depending on bribery as a mechanism for determining the outcome of a sale. I think bribery in international affairs ought to be considered a crime and punishable by imprisonment.

SCHEER: Would you sympathize with the anti-corporate attitude that many voters feel?

CARTER: Well, I'm not particularly anti-corporate, but I'd say I'm more oriented to consumer protection. One of the things I've established throughout the campaign is the need to break up the sweetheart arrangement between regulatory agencies and the industries they regulate. Another is the need for rigid and enthusiastic enforcement of the antitrust laws.

SCHEER: To take another issue, you favor a comprehensive federal health-care system. Why don't you just support the Kennedy-Corman bill, which provides for precisely that?

CARTER: As a general philosophy, wherever the private sector can perform a function as effectively and efficiently as the government, I would prefer to keep it within the private sector. So, I would like the insurance aspect of the health program to be carried out by employer/employee contribution. There would be contributions from the general fund for those who are indigent. I would also have a very heavy emphasis on preventive health care since I believe most of the major afflictions that beset people can be prevented or minimized. And I favor the use to a greater degree of nonphysicians, such as nurses, physician's assistants, and so forth. Some of these things are in conflict with the provisions of the Kennedy-Corman bill.

SCHEER: Let us ask you about one last stand: abortion.

CARTER: I think abortion is wrong and I will do everything I can as president to minimize the need for abortions within the framework of the decision of the Supreme Court, which I can't change. Georgia had a more conservative approach to abortion, which I personally favored, but the Supreme Court ruling suits me all right. I signed a Georgia law as governor that was compatible with the Supreme Court decision.

SCHEER: You think it's wrong, but the ruling suits you? What would we tell a woman who said her vote would depend on how you stood on abortion?

CARTER: If a woman's major purpose in life is to have unrestricted abortions, then she ought *not* to vote for me. But she wouldn't have anyone to vote for.

SCHEER: There seem to have been relatively few women in important staff positions in your campaign. Is that accurate?

CARTER: Women have been in charge of our entire campaign effort in Georgia and New York State outside New York City. Also in Nebraska, Kansas, a third of the state of Florida and other areas.

SCHEER: But whenever we hear about a meeting of top staff members, they almost always seem to be white males. Is that a failing in your organization?

CARTER: I don't know about a failing. The three people with whom I consult regularly—in addition to my wife—are white males: Hamilton Jordan, Jody Powell, and Charles Kirbo. But we do have a lot of women involved in the campaign. We are now setting up a policy committee to run a nationwide effort to coordinate Democratic races and 50 percent of the members of this committee will be women. But Jody has been my press secretary since 1970, and Hamilton and Kirbo were my major advisors in 1966. It's such an extremely stable staff that there's been no turnover at all in the past five or six years. But we've made a lot of progress, I think, in including women, and I think you'll see more.

SCHEER: You mention very frequently how much you count on your wife's advice. Isn't there a strain during the campaign, with the two of you separated so much of the time?

CARTER: Well, when I was in the Navy, I was at sea most of the time and I'd see her maybe one or two nights a week. Now, when I'm home in Plains, I see her almost every night. And if I'm elected president, I'll see her every night. So, there is obviously a time to be together and a time to be separated. If you're apart three or four days and then meet again, it's almost—for me, it's a very exciting reunion. I've been away from Rosalynn for a few days and if I see her across an airport lobby, or across a street, I get just as excited as I did when I was, you know, thirty years younger.

We have a very close, very intimate sharing of our lives and we've had a tremendous magnification of our life's purposes in politics. Before 1966, she and I were both very shy. It was almost a painful thing to approach a stranger or make a speech. It's been a mutual change we've gone through because we both felt it was worthwhile; so, no matter what the outcome of the election, the relationship between Rosalynn and me will be very precious.

SCHEER: Did you both have the usual share of troubles adjusting to marriage?

CARTER: We did at first. We've come to understand each other much better. I was by far the dominant person in the marriage at the beginning, but not anymore. She's just as strong, if not stronger than I am. She's fully equal to me in every way in our relationship, in making business decisions, and she makes most of the decisions about family affairs. And I think it was a struggle for her to achieve this degree of independence and equality in our personal relationship. So, to summarize, years ago we had a lot of quarrels—none serious, particularly—but now we don't.

SCHEER: A lot of marriages are foundering these days. Why is yours so successful?

CARTER: Well, I really love Rosalynn more now than I did when I married her. And I have loved no other women except her. I had gone out with all kinds of girls, sometimes fairly steadily, but I just never cared about them. Rosalynn had been a friend of my sister's and was three years younger than I, which is a tremendous chasm in the high school years. She was just one of those insignificant little girls around the house. Then, when I was twenty-one and home from the Navy on leave, I took her out to a movie. Nothing extraordinary happened, but the next morning I told my mother, "That's the girl I want to marry." It's the best thing that ever happened to me. We also share a religious faith, and the two or three times in our married life when we've had a serious crisis, I think that's what sustained our marriage and helped us overcome our difficulty. Our children, too, have been a factor binding Rosalynn and me together. After the boys, Amy came along late and it's been especially delightful for me, maybe because she's a little girl.

SCHEER: This is a tough question to ask, but because it's been such a factor in American political life, we wonder if you ever discussed with Rosalynn the possibility of being assassinated. And, assuming you have, how do you deal with it in your own mind?

CARTER: Well, in the first place, I'm not afraid of death. In the second place, it's the same commitment I made when I volunteered to go into the submarine force. I accepted a certain degree of danger when I made the original decision, then I didn't worry about it anymore. It wasn't something that preyed on my mind; it wasn't something I had to reassess every five minutes. There is a certain element of danger in running for president, borne out by statistics on the number of presidents who have been attacked, but I have to say frankly that it's something I never worry about.

SCHEER: The first answer was that you don't fear death. Why not?

CARTER: It's part of my religious belief. I just look at death as not a threat. It's inevitable, and I have an assurance of eternal life. There is no feeling on my part that I *have* to be president, or that I *have* to live, or that I'm immune to danger. It's just that the termination of my physical life is relatively insignificant in my concept of overall existence. I don't say that in a mysterious way; I recognize the possibility of assassination. But I guess everybody recognizes the possibility of other forms of death—automobile accidents, airplane accidents, cancer. I just don't worry.

SCHEER: There's been some evidence that Johnson and Nixon both seemed to have gone a bit crazy while they were in the White House. Do you ever wonder if the pressures of the office might make anyone mentally unstable?

CARTER: I really don't have the feeling that being in the White House is what caused Nixon's or Johnson's problems. Other presidents have served without developing mental problems—Roosevelt, Truman, Eisenhower, Kennedy, for instance. As far as I've been able to discern, President Ford approaches—or avoids—the duties of the White House with equanimity and self-assurance.

I think the ability to accept oneself and to feel secure and confident, to avoid any degree of paranoia, to face reality, these factors are fairly independent of whether or not one is president. The same factors would be important if someone were chief of police, or a schoolteacher, or a magazine editor. The pressure is greater on a president, obviously, than some of the jobs I've described, but I think the ability to accommodate pressure is a personal thing.

SCHEER: We noticed your crack about President Ford's avoiding the duties of the White House. Do you agree with Senator Mondale's assessment, when he said shortly after the nomination that Ford isn't intelligent enough to be a good president?

CARTER: Well, if you leave Mondale out of it, I personally think that President Ford is adequately intelligent to be president.

SCHEER: And what about your presidency, if you're elected—will you have a dramatic first one thousand days?

CARTER: I would hope that my administration wouldn't be terminated at the end of one thousand days, as was the case with one administration. I'm beginning to meet with key leaders of Congress to evolve specific legislation to implement the Democratic platform commitment. If I'm elected, there will be no delay in moving aggressively on a broad front to carry out the promises I've made to the American people. I intend to stick to everything I've promised.

SCHEER: Thanks for all the time you've given us. Incidentally, do you have any problems with appearing in *Playboy*? Do you think you'll be criticized?

CARTER: I don't object to that at all. I don't believe I'll be criticized.

(At the final session, which took place in the living room of Carter's home in Plains, the allotted time was up. A press aide indicated that there were other appointments for which Carter was already late, and the aide opened the front door while amenities were exchanged. As the interviewer and the Playboy editor stood at the door, recording equipment in their arms, a final, seemingly casual question was tossed off. Carter then delivered a long, softly spoken monologue that grew in intensity as he made his final points. One of the journalists signaled to Carter that they were still taping, to which Carter nodded his assent.)

SCHEER: Do you feel you've reassured people with this interview, people who are uneasy about your religious beliefs, who wonder if you're going to make a rigid, unbending president?

CARTER: I don't know if you've been to Sunday school here yet; some of the press has attended. I teach there about every three or four weeks. It's getting to be a real problem because we don't have room to put everybody now when I teach. I don't know if we're going to have to issue passes or what. It almost destroys the worship aspect of it. But we had a good class last Sunday. It's a good way to learn what I believe and what the Baptists believe. One thing the Baptists believe is in complete autonomy. I don't accept any domination of my life by the Baptist Church, none. Every Baptist church is individual and autonomous. We don't accept domination of our church from the Southern Baptist Convention. The reason the Baptist Church was formed in this country was because of our belief in absolute and total separation of church and state. These basic tenets make us almost unique. We don't believe in any hierarchy in church. We don't have bishops. Any officers chosen by the church are defined as servants, not bosses. They're supposed to do the dirty work, make sure the church is clean and painted and that sort of thing. So, it's a very good, democratic structure. When my sons were small, we went to church and they went, too. But when they got old enough to make their own decisions, they decided when to go and they varied in their devoutness. Amy really looks forward to going to church, because she gets to see all her cousins at Sunday school. I never knew anything except going to church. My wife and I were born and raised in innocent times. The normal thing to do was to go to church. What Christ taught about most was pride, that one person should never think he was any better than anyone else. One of the most vivid stories Christ told in one of his parables was about two people who went into a church. One was an official of the church, a Pharisee, and he said, "Lord, I thank you that I'm not like all those other people. I keep all your commandments; I give a tenth of everything I own. I'm here to give thanks for making me more acceptable in your sight." The other guy was despised by the nation, and he went in, prostrated himself on the floor and said, "Lord, have mercy on me, a sinner. I'm not worthy to lift my eyes to heaven." Christ asked the disciples which of the two had justified his life. The answer was obviously the one who was humble. The thing that's drummed into us all the time is not to be proud, not to be better than anyone else, not to look down on people but to make ourselves acceptable in God's eyes through our own actions and recognize the simple truth that we're saved by grace. It's just a free gift through faith in Christ. This gives us a mechanism by which we can relate permanently to God. I'm not speaking for other people, but it gives me a sense of peace and equanimity and assurance. I try not to commit a deliberate sin. I recognize that I'm going to do it anyhow because I'm human and I'm tempted. And Christ set some almost impossible standards for us. Christ said, "I tell you that anyone who looks on a woman with lust has in his heart already committed adultery." I've looked on a lot of women with lust. I've committed adultery in my heart many times. This is something that God recognizes I will do—and I have done it—and God forgives me for it. But that doesn't mean I condemn someone who not only looks on a woman with lust but who leaves his wife and shacks up with somebody out of wedlock.

Christ says, don't consider yourself better than someone else because one guy screws a whole bunch of women while the other guy is loyal to his wife. The guy who's loyal to his wife ought not to be condescending or proud because of the relative degree of sinfulness. One thing that Paul Tillich said was that religion is a search for the truth about man's existence and his relationship with God and his fellow man, and that once you stop searching and think you've got it made—at that point, you lose your religion. Consistent reassessment, searching in one's heart—it gives me a feeling of confidence. I don't inject these beliefs in my answers to your secular questions. But I don't think I would ever take on the same frame of mind that Nixon or Johnson did—lying, cheating and distorting the truth. Not taking into consideration my hope for my strength of character, I think that my religious beliefs alone would prevent that from happening to me. I have that confidence. I hope it's justified.

DEBATING OUR DESTINY

INTERVIEW BY JIM LEHRER
PBS NEWSHOUR
APRIL 28, 1989

JIM LEHRER: Mr. President, welcome.

JIMMY CARTER: Thank you, Jim. Good to be with you.

LEHRER: First, in the 1976 debates, you had three with then President Ford. It was his decision to debate you. When he made that decision, was that good news from your standpoint?

CARTER: Well, it was because, as you know, an incumbent president has a lot of advantages, particularly against a relatively unknown governor from Georgia. So, I had been quite successful in the primary season, but it was a very disturbing concept for me to be on the stage with the President of the United States. I'd never even met a Democratic president in my life, so there was an aura about the presidency that was quite overwhelming, but I saw it as a good opportunity to let the people know that I could indeed deal on an equal basis, hopefully, with an incumbent president on matters relating to domestic affairs and defense and foreign policy. I was very excited about it but filled with some trepidation.

LEHRER: But you were ahead in the polls at the time.

CARTER: Yes, but I thought that the concern of the American people was that I had been kind of a flash in the pan. You know, I was able to garner votes within the Democratic party but didn't have knowledge, or intelligence, or background enough to deal with substantive issues. So, I was looking forward to it.

LEHRER: Were you concerned about this problem of being on the stage with a president of the United States and having to defer to him in some way?

CARTER: Yes, I was. I didn't know how to handle it. There was an insecure feeling about being placed, at least for that hour and a half, on an equal basis with the president of our nation. And I had done my background work. I was familiar with the issues. I knew from a governor's experience how to deal with domestic programs. I had been in the Navy for eleven years. I knew a little about defense, and I had been an eager student on international affairs. But I would say that it was one of the most difficult challenges that I had ever faced in my life to be appearing before 70 to 100 million people in the same, on the same level, with the president, yes.

LEHRER: How did you feel going in about your own skills as a debater? Had you done a lot of debating as governor or elsewhere?

CARTER: Well, I had debated in high school and some in college. At the Naval Academy, it's required that you give some after-dinner talks and that you become involved in debates. But that was a very minimal aspect. And in the primary, of course, there were about a dozen of us running against each other, and on many occasions in Iowa and New Hampshire, and then later in the larger states, we had debated each other.

But this format was one that was different, you know, with news—very competent and knowledgeable news reporters asking questions as incisively as they could. But I didn't have any doubt that I had, through the long, tedious, challenging primary months, learned enough about the sensitive issues: how to deal with the Soviet Union, what to do about human rights, how to handle the abortion question, things of that kind. I wasn't ill at ease about my knowledge of a subject.

LEHRER: Did you go in there with a feeling, though, about I can take this guy? I mean, was it a sense of competition about it that evening for that ninety minutes?

CARTER: Yes, it was. This was really the first time I had had a direct confrontation with President Ford, and as a matter of fact, although we were hot competitors, I had an admiration for him because I knew the difficult circumstances under which he had become president. So, there wasn't any personal animosity or vituperation there. There was one of respect for a very worthy opponent, but still a highly competitive atmosphere, and I think I did go in as though it was an athletic competition or a very highly charged competitive arrangement.

LEHRER: Did you do any dry runs in preparation for those '76 debates?

CARTER: Yes, I was thoroughly briefed, and we would emulate the stage setting and have tests just to show how I should react to the presence of the TV cameras, and to try to get my thoughts oriented toward the hundreds of thousands—really tens of millions of people in the TV audience and not just think about the audience that was in the particular theaters where we were. And I can't say that I did it all that well. I was still somewhat ill at ease. I was ill at ease during the debates, but I think the longer that each debate went on, the more I became absorbed in the substance of the issues rather than just afraid that here I am watched by a lot of people, the presidency is at stake.

LEHRER: Was your strategy to show, as you said earlier, that you weren't a flash in the pan, that you were a man of substance, or was it to show that Gerald Ford somehow was not as qualified as you? What was in your mind as your bottom-line objective there?

CARTER: I went in with the full intention just to show that I was indeed of presidential timber and character, not to denigrate or to tear down President Ford. That was my natural inclination, and also among our political advisors, that would have been a very poor political strategy to look as though I was a feisty former governor who was trying to attack the integrity or the competence of an incumbent president. I think it would have been counterproductive. I would have certainly lost the debates if that had happened. So, it was mainly to show my own ability, my own knowledge of the issues, my own character.

LEHRER: There were a couple of specifics on those debates; one of them, you apologized to the people for having granted *Playboy* an interview. Now, did you go into that debate, had you made the decision you were going to say that no matter what the questions were? Or was that something that came to you as you were in the process?

CARTER: Well, we were prepared for that question, I'll put it that way, because, as you know, that *Playboy* interview could have cost me the election. It was a devastating blow to our campaign when this *Playboy* interview was published. The news reporters and the general public just totally forgot about all the issues, what I stood for, what I might do as president when they became absorbed with the *Playboy* interview. So, I was prepared for the question, and I thought the best way to handle it was to say well, I'm sorry that the interview came out, but I couldn't deny that the answers in *Playboy* were my own answers. As a matter of fact, the *Playboy* people had agreed with me and Jody Powell, my press secretary, that they would give us a transcript of the interview and let us approve the transcript before it was published. But when they got the remark about "lust in my heart," it was too juicy an item for them to submit for possible censorship, so they just went ahead and published it, and it really took me aback.

LEHRER: Well, your apology was for using that medium, right . . . for doing the interview with *Playboy*, more than it was what you said?

CARTER: Well, I think "apology" is a little bit . . .

LEHRER: Well, that's my word.

CARTER: It was an expression of regret that I had made a misjudgment.

LEHRER: My point is, you came to say that that night, right?

CARTER: That's right.

LEHRER: And you were going to say it no matter what.

CARTER: The question was inevitable. When you have a media event like that, even a White House press conference in later years, you can anticipate 85 to 90 percent of the questions that are going to be asked, you know, by watching your program, or by reading the *New York Times* or *Washington Post.* You can pretty well say, well, I know these questions are likely to be asked because they are burning issues in the public, and there was no doubt that the *Playboy* interview was a burning issue as it related to me. We knew that question was going to come.

LEHRER: Now, another major thing was in the San Francisco debate when President Ford said, "There is no Soviet domination of Eastern Europe and there never will be under a Ford administration." And there was a follow-up and he kind of repeated it. Did you realize there on the stage that night that President Ford had made a serious mistake?

CARTER: Yes, I did. And I was prepared to jump in, you

know, and take advantage of it. But just on the spur of the moment, I realized that it would serve me better to let the news reporters question President Ford's analysis or his judgment. And so, I didn't have to be on the attack because President Ford, for some strange reason, insisted repeatedly then, and for three or four days later, as a matter of fact, that there was no Soviet domination in Eastern Europe. And this was a very serious mistake that he made, and I don't know if the election turned on it.

LEHRER: I was going to ask you that. Do you think it did?

CARTER: I don't know if it did or not, because there are so many factors that come into a campaign, but certainly it cost him some votes, and as you know, the election was quite close. It may very well have done so, and I think you might say that had it not been for the *Playboy* interview, my margin of victory would have been greater, if President Ford hadn't pardoned President Nixon, you know, who knows what would have happened, or if he had chosen, say, Nelson Rockefeller instead of Bob Dole. There are so many ifs. So many ifs.

LEHRER: Another incident from those debates, the twenty-seven-minute audio failure in Philadelphia. The two of you stood there.

CARTER: I know.

LEHRER: Everyone in America who was watching, you know,

was very, couldn't figure out, this was unreal. What was it like standing there?

CARTER: I watched that tape afterwards and it was embarrassing to me that both President Ford and I stood there almost like robots. We didn't move around; we didn't walk over and shake hands with each other. We just stood there. And it looked very strange, but the fact is that we didn't know at what instant all of the power was going to come back on and the transmissions would be resumed. So, it was a matter of nervousness, kind of. I guess President Ford felt the same way, and said, well, the program is interrupted, is it for ten seconds, or is it for ten minutes? It turned out to be, as you said, twenty-seven minutes.

LEHRER: Were you standing there thinking, "Hey, I ought to go over and talk to this guy, I ought to do something. I ought to yell, 'Hey, what's going on?'"

CARTER: I can't remember exactly. But my recollection is that we were always anticipating that at the next moment, it was going to be over, and then we were going to be right back on live television, and when the cameras were able to transmit again, how were we going to look? So we were, you know, like you are when you [are] getting ready to start a hundred-yard dash and you don't know exactly when the gun is going to be fired, but you get ready, and you don't want to be halfway down the stage when the TV lights come back on. So, I don't know who was more ill at ease, me or President Ford.

LEHRER: It looked like a tie—

CARTER: It was a tie.

LEHRER: —to the audience.

CARTER: Neither one of us was at ease, there's no doubt about that. Those events, I think, to some degree let the American public size up the candidates, and I don't think either one of us made any points on that deal. But I think there has to be a sense of humor, a sense of relaxed attitude towards the cameras, maybe an element of proper generosity toward your opponent, or take advantage of an opening, a demonstration of knowledge about complicated issues, and, of course, some subtle jabs when the opening occurs with an element of humor in them.

LEHRER: Generally speaking, about the '76 debates, how important, taking all three of them, how important do you think they were in your victory?

CARTER: I don't have any way to know. I think they permitted the American people to make a much more informed decision on election day, and whether I actually gained a lot of points or lost a few it's hard to say.

I think the general consensus afterwards was that a couple of them were ties and that I may have won the third one, but who knows, it's a totally subjective sort of thing. I would say that although they may not have affected the outcome of the election more than a few percentage points one way or the other, even not that much, they certainly let the American public size us up better, and I think maybe we in general terms came out a tie.

LEHRER: Let's go to 1980. You had one debate with Ronald Reagan. It was in Cleveland about a week before the election. Did you want that debate, or was that forced on you?

CARTER: I wanted a lot of debates. I wanted three or four debates at least. President Reagan only wanted one debate, and he wanted it as late as possible. And whenever we pursued the subject of the debates, he said, well, we can't have a two-person debate since John Anderson is running as an independent, we've got to have him on as an equal candidate. And obviously, Reagan knew that every time the independent candidate got a vote, it was a vote taken away from me. So, we squabbled back and forth, the assistants did, and finally, President Reagan won that preliminary skirmish, and we only had one debate quite late. I would much have preferred to have at least three debates like President Ford and me.

LEHRER: Why did you want so many debates?

CARTER: Because I thought that I was much more a master of the subject matter. I was much more acquainted with defense, and foreign policy, and domestic issues than he was. Some of his positions on issues were, I thought, unattractive, and my belief was that if we could get down to the substance and get away from the images, that I would come out better. I had watched some tapes of President Reagan on television. I knew that he was a master of the medium, that he was perfectly at ease before the television cameras. I knew that I was not a master of the medium, and I thought that if we'd get past the one hour and go to maybe four, five, six hours on television that substance rather than style would be more prevalent.

LEHRER: But you just had no choice. You were stuck.

CARTER: Well, he just wouldn't debate but once, with me alone, and this was a disappointment to us, but it takes two sides to agree before you can have a debate.

LEHRER: Two memorable happenings in that debate. You said, "I had a discussion with my daughter, Amy, the other day before I came here to ask her what the most important issue was, she said she thought nuclear weaponry." Was that something you had in your mind to say, or did that come to you there on the podium?

CARTER: Well, I had discussed this with my political advisors, not that I would say it, but just the fact that Amy had said it to me, and I was trying to make the point that President Reagan's condemnation of nuclear arms agreements that had been negotiated by Presidents Kennedy and Johnson and Nixon and me were fallacious and that we shouldn't deal with the Soviet Union on this kind of thing. He had made a statement that it was okay with us if Iraq had atomic weapons, things of that kind.

It was important to show that not only I, but all Americans were concerned about a nuclear issue, and I chose the accurate description of a conversation I had had with Amy, hoping that it would prove that this was a matter of great concern. Trying to emphasize the fact that my position on both nuclear arms control issues and nonproliferation was superior to his.

LEHRER: You were ridiculed for it, and you were criticized for it. Did you expect that? Were you surprised?

CARTER: I was surprised. But President Reagan and his political advisers turned it around to I think his advantage by saying that I was getting my advice on nuclear power issues or arms control issues from my teenage daughter. And it was used by the Republicans to ridicule me, and I think they probably gained some political points from it.

LEHRER: When you look back on that, do you look upon that as a mistake you made?

CARTER: Yes, I think so. It was an honest statement that made a point that still is remembered. I got a flood of letters afterwards, you know, "Congratulations. You did the right thing. Your daughter Amy had more judgment about nuclear weaponry than Reagan did," and so forth. But I think in the contest there just a few days before the election, he came out ahead on that deal.

LEHRER: The other thing that's remembered about that debate is when he said, "There you go again." There was reaction in the hall, I recall. What was your reaction when he said that? It's mentioned all the time, as you know.

CARTER: I know. Well, I'm sure that was a well-rehearsed line that President Reagan had prepared carefully, the style of delivery when he would bring it in, and it was an inevitable statement that he would make. I don't even remember the comment that I made that he chose to tag that statement to. But that was a memorable line and I think it showed that he was relaxed and had a sense of humor, and it was kind of a denigrating thing to me. And I think that he benefited from saying that, politically speaking.

When the debate was over, I really felt good about it, and when my staff and I went down into the little holding room before a reception, we were celebrating, you know, the victory of the debate. I think ABC has a quick follow-up poll, a call-in telephone poll, and you had to pay fifty cents to make a call in and according to the telephone poll, President Reagan won the debate, and the big head-lines were "Reagan Wins Debate" as determined by the ABC call-in poll, or whatever it was. We rationalized the outcome by saying that not enough Democrats had fifty cents to spend on the telephone poll, that it was stacked against poor Democrats. But who knows? The debate was not a victory for me, but I still think that if you analyze the debate or listen to it on the radio, or see a transcript, there's no doubt that I won. But if you look at the televi-sion play of it, I think it's accurate for me to say or admit that Reagan won.

LEHRER: Mr. Reagan himself said, "The debate with President Carter was, in my view, a critical element in our success in the election."

CARTER: Well, I can't deny that. You have to remember that President Reagan won by less than 51 percent of the votes. It wasn't an overwhelming mandate for him. And I am convinced, and I was then, that a week before the election we were neck and neck. It could have gone either way.

The turning . . . the major factor in the election had nothing to do with the debate. It was a fact that we went through election day, which was the exact one-year anniversary of the hostages being taken in Iran. There was a flurry of activity in the Iranian Parliament, that they were going to vote on whether or not to release the hostages just before the votes were cast in this country. The Parliament decided under Khomeini's pressure that they would not release the hostages, and this devastating, negative news about hostages swept the country on election day. I've always been convinced that this was a major factor.

LEHRER: And the debate really didn't play that much a part?

CARTER: I don't think so, no.

LEHRER: Let's talk generally then about presidential debates. Based on your experience and your observations of others, do you think they should be a required part of the presidential election process?

CARTER: Yes, I do. I may be one of the few that thinks so. It would suit me fine to see the Congress pass a law even that would provide for a series of debates and how they would be sponsored, and approximately when they would be held so that there wouldn't be this inevitable squabble every four years: are we going to have debates, who is going to sponsor them, when will they be, how many will there be, what format will there be, and things like that. I think it would be very good to set up this sort of thing, maybe with a responsible objective, fair, unbiased kind of sponsorship, and then take all the guesswork out of it, and let the American people know that no matter who their candidates are, say in 1992, that there are going to be three debates. They will be held, say, two, four, and six weeks before election day, and they will be sponsored by maybe national public television or somebody like that. I would like to see that done.

LEHRER: Why? Why are they important?

CARTER: I think the American people, particularly in 1988, saw a gross, even embarrassing misuse of the media by the candidates with distorted television spots, and emphasis on issues that were not substantive, and there are very few opportunities really for the nominees of the two parties to demonstrate to the American people their capabilities, and to let the news media who might be the interrogators, I presume, bring to the forefront issues that might actually be significant once a president is in office. And I don't know of a different format within which this can be assured or guaranteed. This past year was the worst, I think, certainly in electronic history, with distortions and character attacks and the avoidance of substantive issues. I think the debates would almost ensure that that doesn't happen again.

LEHRER: But there were two presidential debates in 1988. Did you see those two?

CARTER: Yes, of course.

LEHRER: What did you think?

CARTER: I saw one of them. I was in Africa for the other.

LEHRER: What was your reaction?

CARTER: I thought they were beneficial, and I would like to see this kind of institutionalized, maybe even by law.

LEHRER: Do you think there is a connection, then, between debating skill and being president of the United States?

CARTER: Yes, there is certainly a connection. Because one of the major roles of a president is to communicate ideas, concepts, concerns, dreams, ambitions or facts to the American people. It's about the only way you have to gather support for programs that you think are significant for our country when there are massive opposing forces, say, focused on the Congress. And I think to get the public on your side, or to explain a difficult issue, or to acknowledge a mistake, or to spell out a circumstance is very important. And I think if a president can't communicate well, then in some ways that president is handicapped in doing a good job.

LEHRER: And a debate would expose that to the American people.

CARTER: I think so, and it also, it also makes the candidates realize how important this ability to communicate is. I think it has nothing but beneficial effects.

LEHRER: And, when you use the word "debate," you are using the word the way I'm using it, the way everybody does, it's kind of a joint appearance. You think the candidates ought to be required to speak together on the same platform about the same issues, is that correct?

CARTER: Yes, that's right.

LEHRER: You don't have a particular format in mind.

CARTER: No. I think the general format that has been used is acceptable, where the reporters ask one candidate a question and the candidate answers, and then the other candidate has a right to respond, and then maybe a brief second follow-up response from the original candidate, and then reverse the procedure with the other candidate. That kind of thing I think lets them have an adequate opportunity to respond to a substantive question from the news media, and then have a little exchange between the two. I think that's adequate.

LEHRER: Mr. President, thank you very much.

CARTER: Thank you. I enjoyed it.

COLD WAR: BACKYARD

INTERVIEWER UNKNOWN
NATIONAL SECURITY ARCHIVE
CNN
1989

INTERVIEWER: The Middle East, first of all, Mr. Carter. What led you to propose reconvening the Geneva talks?

JIMMY CARTER: Well, I had an interest in the Middle East from the time I was much younger, and then when I was governor, I went to the Middle East to travel around—that was in 1972. During my campaign for president, I made it clear to the American people, and I guess to the warriors who would listen, that when I became the leader of this country, that I would initiate the strongest possible move to bring peace to the Middle East. As you know, nothing was being done then on the peace front. UN Resolution 242 had been passed, but nothing had happened. So, very early in my term, beginning in January, I began to invite the various leaders to come to Washington and to meet with me: President Rabin, who was prime minister of Israel at that time; King Hussein came over; President Sadat came over; later Menachem Begin came over after he was elected in May, I think. Assad has never yet been to the United States, so I met him in Geneva. During a G7 meeting in London, I went over to Geneva to meet with Assad. So, by the time the end of the first five months had passed of my term, I had met with all the key leaders in the Middle East. And I felt, after talking to Sadat in particular, that that was a time to reinitiate a strong move, led by me, for a peace effort. Then it seemed that I should do it completely within the framework of the UN resolutions, Security Council resolutions, and that was my hope. In response to my conversations with him, Sadat first decided that he would invite all the participants to come to Cairo, including all the five nations, the prominent members of the Security Council. I was very averse to bring in France and China, as well as Great Britain and the United States, so I objected to that and suggested that he have another alternative in mind, and that's when he decided to go directly to Jerusalem.

INTERVIEWER: In an important speech that you made early that year, you talked about the necessity to introduce fairness into a settlement in the Middle East. What did you mean by that?

CARTER: Well, this speech got me into a lot of trouble because I talked about a homeland for the Palestinians. Prior to that time, and maybe since then as well, the United States government policy has been overwhelmingly oriented toward compatibility with the government in Jerusalem, in Israel, and I felt that we couldn't really make progress in bringing about a comprehensive peace between Israel and her Arab neighbors without at least addressing the concerns of the Palestinians, of Egypt and of Jordan in particular. So, in that speech that I made, I think in Massachusetts, I thought that it was proper to say that the Palestinians deserved a homeland of their own, and this aroused a furor in some circles in my country; but it was a necessary prerequisite for the further progress that was made between Israel and Egypt.

INTERVIEWER: After Sadat's visit to Jerusalem and speech to the Knesset, and after a great deal more hard work, you managed to get the major participants to come to Camp David to sit down with you. How difficult were those thirteen days?

CARTER: I think, as everyone will probably remember, when Sadat went to Jerusalem it was a momentous event. He made a very harsh speech to the Israeli Knesset, but the fact that he went there and made a speech did away with the sharp edges of what he actually said. Later, when he and Begin had a meeting in Ismailia, they were totally incompatible; they were only together fifteen minutes or so, and then they separated in some degree of anger. I had my hopes up when Sadat went to Jerusalem, and my hopes in effect were dashed when the results were so poor. So it was that failure of real progress after Sadat's historic trip that caused me to invite Begin and Sadat to come to Camp David, which I did with a long handwritten personal letter to each one, and they both accepted. I didn't know what was going to happen at Camp David—no one knew—and I think the general presumption was that not much would happen. And at the time, we envisioned maybe three days of exploratory talks. When I arrived at Camp David, Sadat followed me first, and Sadat was willing to comply with my hope that we might elevate our expectations dramatically and actually have an agreement between Israel and Egypt. When Begin came, though, he wanted us just to do some preparations for future talks that would go into any kind of details with the foreign ministers and defense ministers at some neutral place in the Middle East. And so it was out of that environment that we began our negotiations. The first three days of the talks were very unpleasant: primarily, I and Begin and Sadat in a very small room. Sometimes the secretary of state, Cyrus Vance, was there. I would try to get the two men to agree on something, and they couldn't agree on anything; they were very antagonistic. No matter what my efforts were, they always wanted to revert back to what had happened in the last twenty-five years, with four wars and boys killed and bombs dropped. So, for the last ten days in Camp David, they never saw each other. I kept them totally apart, and I went back and forth between the Egyptians and the Israelis to try to conclude an agreement. I used then, and still use, a technique that I call "the single document technique," in that I have exactly the same text that I present to the Israelis and the Egyptians, and every time one of them insists on a change, I make that change and present it to the other, so there's no reason for them to believe that I'm misleading them. And so it was that long, tedious, back-and-forth negotiation that finally brought the two men to an agreement.

INTERVIEWER: You didn't get much sleep?

CARTER: No, I didn't get much sleep, but there was an element of excitement and . . . you know, there that kept us going.

INTERVIEWER: But how near did the talks come to complete breakdown at the end?

CARTER: Almost completely, on two occasions. One was when Sadat met with Moshe Dayan, whom he had hardly known. Moshe Dayan was foreign minister then. He had known Ezer Weizmann quite well and liked Weizmann. But he had a talk with Dayan, and Dayan in effect, without my knowing it, told Sadat, "The Israelis will go no further; there will be no more concessions on the part of the Israelis." I didn't know it, but Sadat told the Egyptian delegation, "We are leaving Camp David," and he went to my national security adviser, Zbigniew Brzezinski, and said, "Bring my helicopter—I'm going back to Egypt." I learned about this, and I went over to Sadat's cabin, and I confronted him in a very frank and ultimately successful way. I said that "our friendship is over. You promised me that you would stay at Camp David as long as I was willing to negotiate, and here you have made your plans to leave without even consulting me, and I consider this a serious blow to our personal friendship and to the relationship between Egypt and the United States." And he agreed to stay, to the consternation of the other Egyptians. That was one time it almost broke down. And the other time was at the end of the talks, when Begin had made an oath before God that he would never dismantle an Israeli settlement, and there was a substantial settlement on Egyptian territory, called Yamit; about three thousand Israelis were there. Begin could not bring himself to violate his promise to God. So, at the last minute, we evolved an alternative: that Begin would stand aside and let the Israeli parliament, the Knesset, decide to dismantle or not dismantle the settlement. And after that, we signed the Camp David Accords, and then later the Knesset voted 85 percent to dismantle the settlement at Yamit. To my disappointment, they not only withdrew the Israeli settlers, but they also bulldozed everything level with the ground.

INTERVIEWER: Those accords—one of your greatest achievements?

CARTER: I would say one of the achievements. I don't know whether they have the longest-lasting impact. Some of the domestic legislation—we deregulated almost everything in the government, and we had the bill, and I normalized relations with the People's Republic of China and had the Panama Canal treaties. But certainly, that was one of the highlights of my administration, yes.

INTERVIEWER: I'd like to turn to human rights, for which you'll very certainly always be remembered, for your belief in that. You said very early on that human rights would be a fundamental tenet of your foreign policy. Why did you say that, and what does that mean?

CARTER: I come out of the environment of the Deep South, where I had seen the millstone of racial discrimination weighting down my people, both the Black people and the white people; and I had seen the enormous progress that we were able to make after we removed the legal restraints of a two-class society, with the whites superior and Blacks inferior. So, I was very convinced before I became President that basic human rights, equality of opportunity, the end of abuse by governments of their people, was a basic principle on which the United States should be an acknowledged champion. So, I made the statement even before I was inaugurated, as has been said, that . . . I announced that human rights would be a cornerstone or foundation of our entire foreign policy. So, I officially designated every US ambassador on earth to be my personal human rights representative, and to have the embassy be a haven for people who suffered from abuse by their own government. And every time a foreign leader met with me, they knew that human rights in their country would be on the agenda. And . . . I think that this was one of the seminal changes that was brought to US policy. And although, in the first few weeks of his term, my successor Ronald Reagan disavowed this policy and sent an emissary down to Argentina and to Chile and to Brazil, to the military dictators, and said, "The human rights policy of Carter is over," it was just a few months before he saw that the American people supported this human rights policy and that it was good for his administration, so after that, he became a strong protector of human rights as well.

INTERVIEWER: But relationships between states are based partly—some would say largely—on realpolitik. The Soviet Union regarded your constant addressing of the issue of human rights in relation to them as a sort of provocation. Were you prepared for that? Did that concern you? Did it help your foreign policy or hinder it?

CARTER: That's hard to say. There's another word that may not be in the dictionary: "idealpolitik," real and ideal. I didn't single out the Soviet Union for my human rights policy: I applied it in a much more difficult way to the regimes in South America, most of which were military dictatorships and very abusive. But the Soviet leaders did assume that my human rights policy was targeted against them, to embarrass them. I don't have any regrets about having done so. There's no doubt that this was a cause of disharmony between me and Brezhnev, between my secretary of state and Gromyko and so forth. But it resulted almost immediately in a dramatic increase, for instance, in Jewish migration from the Soviet Union. The first year I was in office, only about eight hundred people came out of the Soviet Union: Jews. By the third year I was in office . . . second year, 1979, fifty-one thousand came out of the Soviet Union. And every one of the human rights heroes—I'll use the word—who have come out of the Soviet Union, have said it was a turning point in their lives, and not only in the Soviet Union but also in places like Czechoslovakia and Hungary and Poland [they] saw this human rights policy of mine as being a great boost to the present democracy and freedom that they enjoy. I don't want to exaggerate its effect, but I think it was a very sound policy, and it's basically been followed since then, and I think there's a much more intense awareness of human rights principles now than there would have been otherwise.

INTERVIEWER: Historians today would say that the pressures that you helped engender within those societies led to the crack-up or helped to lead to the crack-up of the Communist system at the end of the Cold War.

CARTER: Well, there's no doubt about that, that the American human rights policy greatly strengthened the democratic forces that were in their embryonic or infant stage in many countries around the world, and I would say particularly within the Soviet bloc.

INTERVIEWER: Agreed. President Carter, I'd like to talk to you now about arms. When you came to office, you immediately began to press for deep cuts in arms levels. Why did you do that?

CARTER: I thought it was necessary. I issued directives, for instance, not only considering nuclear weapons but also sophisticated so-called . . .

INTERVIEWER: I wonder if I could interrupt you and ask you to start that answer again and say, "To me, it was very important that we should achieve a reduction . . ."

CARTER: OK, that's good. You interrupt me whenever.

INTERVIEWER: Yeah.

CARTER: Well, one of the greatest concerns that I had when I became president was the vast array of nuclear weapons in the arsenals of the United States and the Soviet Union and a few other countries, and, also the great proliferation of conventional weapons, nonnuclear weapons, particularly as a tremendous burden on the economies of developing or very poor countries. So, I did a few things: I issued a directive, which is still in effect now, prohibiting the sale of any sophisticated weaponry to any country in this hemisphere, and that involves F-16s or F-15s or advanced aircraft. It's still in effect. The other thing I did was to try to put forward to the Soviet Union a much more dramatic reduction in the total quantity and effectiveness of the nuclear weapons in our arsenals, and to bring about a comprehensive test ban to eliminate the explosion of any nuclear devices, either underground or in the air. And as is well-known, in March of the first year I was in office, I sent my secretary of state, Cy Vance, to Moscow with what I thought was a very good proposal for dramatic cuts, but as an alternative, just to continue an evolutionary step-by-step move from the Vladivostok agreement that my predecessor Gerald Ford had negotiated. The response in Moscow was not very favorable.

INTERVIEWER: I mean, coming so soon after Vladivostok, Brezhnev was obviously quite worried by what you were proposing.

CARTER: Yes, he was. And in retrospect, I can see that President Brezhnev was quite proud of the limited agreement that he had concluded in Vladivostok; and to have a new American president come in and say, "That is not good enough—let's do much more, and do it quite rapidly," took him by surprise.

INTERVIEWER: When the Soviet Union introduced SS-20 missiles into the European theater, as it were, you saw that as a serious threat.

CARTER: Yes, this was a form . . . The SS-20 that the Soviets introduced into the European theater, was a new and unexpected and very formidable weapon. It had large warheads, it had three warheads, and the weapons were mobile: they could be moved up and down on railroad tracks so that we never knew exactly where they were; and they were designed primarily to hit nearby targets throughout Europe, including Great Britain. And so, the previously negotiated nuclear arms agreement had not really referred directly to these kinds of fairly short-range missiles—they were long enough. So, I did look upon them as a great threat to stability, and we had primarily addressed, earlier than that, the enormous intercontinental missiles that had been on the table for discussion primarily between President Nixon and the Soviet Union.

INTERVIEWER: But did you find it easy to get your European allies—I'm thinking particularly of Helmut Schmidt— to accept that Pershing missiles, for example, should be introduced into the theater in response to the SS-20s?

CARTER: Well, we didn't have much of an altercation between me and European leaders, including Helmut Schmidt, concerning Pershing missiles, but we did have an altercation concerning the neutron weapon. The neutron weapon was something about which we had the technology. It was designed not to destroy buildings and tanks but destroy human beings by the penetrating force of the nuclear waste products from the explosion. It was an antipersonnel weapon. Earlier, before I became president, a commitment had been made that the United States would proceed with the development of this missile; but when we got down to the point of expending large sums of money in developing the neutron weapon, it became obvious to me that no leader in Europe was willing to agree to deploy these weapons on their territory. And despite my efforts to get Helmut Schmidt and Jim Callaghan in Great Britain to do so, they would never agree. I had serious qualms about this missile anyway since it was inherently antipersonnel and not anti-tank or anti-building, so I canceled the project, and there was some altercation between me and the German chancellor about the way that I did this.

INTERVIEWER: What was achieved at the Vienna summit in 1979?

CARTER: Well, the Vienna summit was in 1980. You may want to ask a question because in '79 we went . . . Oh, you mean with Brezhnev?

INTERVIEWER: Yeah.

CARTER: OK, I'll give you another answer. I was thinking about the G7. OK. In 1979, we had a very productive summit between me and Brezhnev to negotiate the terms of the SALT II nuclear weapons agreement. He and I got along quite well. It was a harmonious meeting. I assuaged his concerns about my recent normalizing of diplomatic relations with China. That had been the cause of great consternation in Moscow, because they could envision, in their somewhat paranoid state, that the US and China were secretly ganging up against the Soviet Union. This was not the case. I think I alleviated his concerns with my discussions with him. In addition to that, we put reasonable limits on the size of our nuclear arsenals, agreeing to dismantle or destroy certain weapons. And expecting a future negotiation to go further than that, we also put a five-year limit on the effectiveness of the SALT II treaty. As a matter of fact, history will show that it lasted indefinitely, and President Reagan only announced that it would be terminated at the end of seven years, so it lasted longer than it was supposed to do. I was prepared . . . So, one of the things that I might add quickly is that when a president negotiates an agreement of this kind, it goes into effect because the president has the ability to control the nuclear arsenal to some degree. The Congress never did ratify this treaty, although I presented it to the Congress, to the committee, Foreign Relations Committee, because that winter, just six months later, the Soviet Union invaded Afghanistan, and at that time it would have been almost impossible to get the Congress and the American public to approve anything that related to commonality with the Soviet Union after they invaded Afghanistan.

INTERVIEWER: At the end of your term of office, having come into power hoping to reduce arms expenditure, you had to increase it in various important ways. Did that mean that in your view détente was over and confrontation was on again? Why were you forced to change your grand strategy in that way?

CARTER: Well, I didn't really change my grand strategy when I reduced the constraints on our own capability militarily, and so, over a period of my term in office, each year we had some increase in defense expenditures. The problem was that before I became president, in the aftermath of the Vietnam War, there had been fairly dramatic, and I think excessive, reductions in the capability of our military forces, and as a former military man myself—I was a professional naval officer, a submarine officer—I thought it was better, on a step-by-step, very carefully planned way, to increase the technical, or technological, capability of our weapons systems. So, I chose as my secretary of defense Harold Brown, a distinguished physicist who had been considered for a Nobel Prize in physics, the head of California Institute of Technology, one of the finest engineering schools on earth. And it was Harold Brown's technical ability as secretary of defense that let us develop all the advanced weapons that were later demonstrated in the Gulf War when President Bush was in office. So, my . . . my thrust was to make sure that the American military was lean, was as small as possible, but had the highest capability of advanced technology. This included, for instance, the highly publicized stealth aircraft, which at that time was our best-kept secret.

INTERVIEWER: So, in fact, again, the policies that you inaugurated towards the end of your term had a lasting influence on America's stance in the Cold War, until the end of the war?

CARTER: Yes, there's no doubt about it. And the fact that we developed . . . and I even announced, during my last year in office, that we had developed the technology for the stealth aircraft, which makes them totally impervious to any sort of defense—there's no way to see them in the sky with radar—and so I don't think there's any doubt about that. And then, after he came into office, as you know, President Reagan even escalated the amount of money spent for defense, I think excessively, because he went back and resurrected some of the weapons systems, the big bombers that were already outdated and were just designed primarily to create employment opportunities in California.

INTERVIEWER: If I could stay on arms and go back to your message to Brezhnev in '77, the letter you sent him in February, and the visit of Cy Vance to Moscow in March. What was your reaction when Brezhnev . . . can you remember what you felt, what you thought, what you did, when Brezhnev appeared so surprised and dismayed and critical?

CARTER: Well, I was taken aback, and I think the . . . Let me start over again. When I sent the secretary of state, Cy Vance, to Moscow in . . . early in 1977, and the Soviet Union rejected our nuclear disarmament proposal so vehemently, I was really surprised. And I have to say, I think accurately, that we gave Brezhnev two alternatives. One was the step-by-step evolutionary reductions, based on Vladivostok; and the other one was a much more dramatic and quick reduction in the total arsenals that we took to him. But he had the option of taking either one. As a matter of fact, they reacted very negatively to this proposal. And when Foreign

Minister Gromyko came out of the Kremlin and made his public statement, he almost ignored the subject of nuclear weapons: he concentrated on a vituperative attack concerning our human rights policy and alleged—incorrectly—that our human rights policy was designed to embarrass the Soviet Union and was a confrontational effort on my part. So, I would say that their rejection of our more bold nuclear arms control proposal was more designed as an adverse reaction to our human rights policy than it was to the substance of the military proposal.

INTERVIEWER: What was Brezhnev like?

CARTER: Well, I only met Brezhnev in June of 1979, in Vienna. He was ill. It was his time to come to Washington, but he was constrained by his doctors not to fly at any great altitude because of his ear problem, so he could only fly short distances; so, I agreed, very generously and easily to go to Vienna instead. He had to be supported as he walked around . . . by someone; he was obviously unbalanced in his walking—he had an inner-ear problem. But he was very alert mentally, and he was very harmonious with me. We had long talks, privately, just the two of us, with interpreters, about all kinds of issues—I mentioned our normalized relations with China; we had a good talk about human rights policy. He was proud of the number of Jews who were being permitted to leave the Soviet Union. We had reached agreement on the SALT II treaty; we had laid plans for future, more dramatic reductions, and so forth. And one of the surprising things that Brezhnev said when we were in our talks was—when I proposed that we make these changes in nuclear weaponry, he said, "God will never forgive us if we don't succeed." And, you know, coming from the leader of an atheistic Communist country, this surprised everyone. I think the most surprised person at the table was Gromyko, who looked up at the sky like this and did his hands in a peculiar way, as though this was a shocking thing for Brezhnev to say. But I would repeat that Brezhnev and I were quite compatible. And I don't know how strong he was at home. Chernenko was with him, and the military leaders were with him, and Gromyko was with him. I felt that all of them were much more . . . I'd say cautious or conservative than was Brezhnev. And it was only . . . that was June, and in December, right after Christmas, was when they invaded Afghanistan, and that's when the good progress that we were making was fairly well made impossible for a while.

INTERVIEWER: Why did SALT II arouse such strong feeling in the United States, such critical feeling in the United States?

CARTER: Well, as a matter of fact, it didn't. When we first negotiated SALT II, there was a general acceptance of the success that we had in Vienna; and over a period of time—it always takes a few months—we got the documents in proper shape, with the backup legislation to present to the Congress for ratification. It takes a two-thirds vote in the US Senate. But about the time they got ready to vote on SALT II is when the Soviets invaded Afghanistan, and then this totally wiped out any possibility for agreement between us and the Soviet Union. But as I've said earlier, the terms of the SALT II treaty were enforceable by me and Brezhnev independent of US Senate ratification, so the SALT II treaty was completely honored throughout its life.

INTERVIEWER: Just to go back once more to Camp David, could you say what you think the effect of those accords were on the progress of the Cold War? Is there a relationship between what you achieved in the Middle East and a broader international situation?

CARTER: It's hard for me to see a direct connection between the Camp David Accords and the peace that was signed later between Israel and Egypt. On the overall Cold War situation, the Soviet Union at that time had two major investments: one was in Syria, which was kind of their entrée to the Middle East process; and the other one was more indirectly through the PLO. I was dealing very harmoniously not only with Israel and Egypt, but also Jordan and Saudi Arabia and other Middle East countries, so I don't really think there was ever any confrontation or aspect of confrontation between the Soviet Union and the United States because of the Camp David peace effort. As you know, however, under President Nixon, when the Israelis were in the war in the early seventies and crossed the Suez and started toward Cairo, the Soviets marshaled their nuclear forces and put them on extreme alert and notified President Nixon: "If the Israelis don't stop their advance, we will intercede militarily on the side of Egypt." So that's when the confrontation came between the US and the Soviet Union concerning the Middle East.

INTERVIEWER: What price did Sadat pay for the Middle East accords?

CARTER: Hmm . . . Well, Sadat, who is the leader I most admire that I've ever met, was a man of great personal courage and wisdom and generosity, and he was quite knowledgeable about the broad aspects of diplomacy on a global basis. Sadat was a little bit too self-assured, a little maybe too free of concern about what his neighbors thought. He would sometimes make derogatory remarks about the royal family in Saudi Arabia, and I would caution him, "Don't say this because, you know, they're part of the people that most support you." He anticipated, I think, at Camp David that if the accords were signed, that Egypt would suffer from an economic boycott of sorts from the other Arab countries. I don't think that he anticipated as severe a boycott effort or an embargo on trade as did materialize, but he was willing to accept this. And of course, I think he also underestimated the animosity toward him personally within his own country, and this was demonstrated tragically when he was assassinated by his own people as his own military troops went in front of the reviewing stand. The loss of Sadat was a tragic blow to peace in the Middle East, and I think to global stability.

INTERVIEWER: And it was a personal blow to you and Mrs. Carter.

CARTER: One of the saddest days of my life, almost equivalent to the death of my own father or my own brothers and sisters, was the death of Anwar Sadat.

INTERVIEWER: Iran—when the Shah was deposed, was that a blow to the United States?

CARTER: Yes, it was; it was a blow to the United States when the Shah was deposed. He had been a close associate, an ally with, I think if I'm not mistaken, seven presidents who preceded me, and we never dreamed that the Shah was likely to be overthrown by his own people. But when he became embattled by attacks from his own people at home, and particularly from the Ayatollah Khomeini, who was issuing broadcasts and tape recordings from France, we gave the Shah every possible legitimate support. When he was finally overthrown and had to leave the country, we tried to find him a haven where he could reside, and he eventually wound up in Panama, without any one of us knowing that he had terminal cancer, which was revealed later on. During the interim period, after the Shah was forced out of Iran into exile, during the first ten or eleven months of 1979, we had a working relationship with his revolutionary replacement. We helped them find accommodations in Washington for their diplomatic staff and so forth, and they were paying bills to American contractors that had been incurred under the Shah, and so forth. It was only in November, the first week in November, when the students, militants took over the American embassy, that the situation deteriorated. And before I let the Shah come to New York for treatment for his cancer, I had direct assurances from the president and the prime minister of Iran, from Bazargan and Yazdi, were their names, that if the Shah would come to New York for treatment and not make any political statements, that they would assure me that the American interests in Iran would be protected. While they were still in office, American hostages were taken, and our embassy was overrun. Two or three days later, the Ayatollah Khomeini's son went into the embassy and in effect endorsed positively what the students or militants had done. Bazargan and Yazdi resigned in protest, and then we were faced with the long period of holding our hostages. But we had tried successfully to get along with the revolutionary government after the Shah was overthrown. We tried to sustain the Shah as long as he said he had a chance of staying there; we provided a haven for him to go to after he was put into exile, and I permitted him to come to New York for treatment for his terminal cancer.

INTERVIEWER: Mr. Carter, could you have anticipated that the staff of the embassy would have been seized and made hostages?

CARTER: Well, I was taken aback by surprise when the militants overran our embassy and captured our hostages and then refused to release them. First of all, this is contrary to the basic Islamic faith. The Koran says you must protect foreign emissaries when they're in your country; in a religious sense, this was a violation of the Islamic law. And I had been given full assurance before I let the Shah come to New York for treatment, that American interests would be protected in Iran. The president and prime minister—Bazargan and Yazdi were their names—gave me this assurance. After the

militants took the American embassy and captured our
hostages, the president and prime minister of Iran resigned in
protest against this violation of their commitment. So, I was
obviously surprised when this occurred.

INTERVIEWER: Were the hostages, in your view, deliberately
not released, in spite of all your efforts, until after Ronald
Reagan was sworn in as president?

CARTER: Yes, I believe that's the case. Well, I'd better start
over again. The first thing I did after the hostages were taken,
was to send the Ayatollah Khomeini a secret message: "If
you put any of our hostages on trial, I will [interfere in] all
commerce between Iran and the outside world. If you injure
or kill a hostage, I will respond militarily." And after that, the
ayatollah never made any statements about injuring or killing
a hostage or putting any on trial, so I felt that the hostages'
lives were being protected. We tried many times, through
all kinds of emissaries—Germany, France, Syria, the PLO,
Muhammad Ali, to get the hostages released, unsuccessfully.
And I think certainly, toward the end of my term, when
we could have had the hostages released, that the ayatollah
deliberately delayed their release until five minutes after I
was no longer president. The morning of the inauguration of
President Reagan, when I went out of office, the hostages had
been sitting in an airplane at the end of the runway into Iran
for several hours, waiting to take off, and they waited until I
was no longer president.

INTERVIEWER: You've explained the long relationship of

partnership or clientship or friendship between the United States and Iran under the Shah. Did you tell him, when you were in office, what you thought of his record on human rights?

CARTER: Yes, very strongly. When the Shah was in Washington for a state visit in November of 1977, his secret police, SAVAK, had fired into a crowd of peaceful demonstrators and killed, I believe, several hundred of them. When the Shah came to visit me, I took him aside into a small office that I had adjacent to the Oval Office, and I told him that I thought that he was making a serious mistake in violating the human rights of his own people through his secret police and in taking strong military action against peaceful demonstrators. I advised him strongly not to do this any further. He replied to me with some degree of scorn and said that not only the United States, but all the European countries were making a serious mistake in permitting demonstrations of our people against our government, that this was obviously a Communist plot to overthrow democracy and freedom in the Western world, and we were ignorant as leaders in not stamping out this kind of demonstration at its earliest stage. And he said that . . . in the nation of Iran, there were just a tiny handful of people who opposed his regime, and these were all Communists, inspired and controlled from outside, that there was no indigenous threat to his popularity. That was his response. It was a very frank and fairly unpleasant confrontation but in private.

INTERVIEWER: What forewarning did you have of the Soviet invasion of Afghanistan?

CARTER: I had no forewarning in Christmas week of 1979 that the Soviets were going to invade Afghanistan. I was deeply concerned about Iran: there was a burgeoning animosity between Iran and Iraq; the Iranian stability was quite fragile. Pakistan was adjacent to Afghanistan, and I could see that the Soviet movement into Afghanistan was not an end in itself. The intelligence that I had from various sources, including within the Soviet Union, was that the Soviets' long-term goal was to penetrate into access to warmwater oceans from Afghanistan, either through Iran or through Pakistan. I saw this as a direct threat to global stability and to the security of my own nation. I had several alternatives, one of which was military action, which I thought was out of the question halfway around the world, with the powerful Soviet military adjacent to Afghanistan. So, I exhausted all the other means that I had to put restraints on the Soviet Union. One of them was to issue a public statement that if the Soviets did invade either Pakistan or Iran out of Afghanistan, that I would consider this a personal threat [to] the security of the United States of America and I would take whatever action I desired or considered appropriate to respond, and I let it be known that this would not exclude a nuclear reaction. This was a very serious and sobering statement that I made, and I relayed this in more private terms to Brezhnev and encouraged him to restrain the Soviet forces and urged him to withdraw them from Afghanistan.

INTERVIEWER: Could you just say where you were when you got the news, and what you did on the twenty-seventh of December 1979?

CARTER: Yes. In December of 1979, I was in Washington, although I would have normally been in my home in Plains, Georgia, for Christmas with my family, but since the hostages were being held at that time and I was making every effort on a daily basis, twenty-four hours a day potentially, to explore every possibility for their release, I did not go home for Christmas. So, I was in my normal quarters as president in Washington, and sometimes back and forth to Camp David, when the Soviets—

INTERVIEWER: I think you got the news in Camp David, didn't you, on the twenty-seventh of December?

CARTER: Yes, I was at Camp David. On the twenty-seventh of December, I was in Camp David, but you have to remember that my communications setup and my access to the outside world and to the government was the equivalent in Camp David to what it was in the White House, and it's only a short helicopter flight between the two. So, I was, you might say, on duty as president and not on vacation when the Soviets invaded Afghanistan.

INTERVIEWER: What sort of message did you send Brezhnev the following day on the hotline, the telex hotline?

CARTER: I sent Brezhnev an inquiry. At first: "What are your intentions in invading Afghanistan? Uh, when will you withdraw?" That was my first question. He sent me word back that he had been invited into Afghanistan, to maintain stability there, by Afghan leaders. The fact is that as his forces went into Afghanistan, he carried in a puppet leader that he implanted in Kabul to administer the government that was to be controlled by the Soviet Union. I knew that his response was not honest. Then they continued to pour in airplane after airplane loaded with troops, and then to cross the border on land as well. This took several days. That's when I decided to issue my statement, that I've already described, that I considered any further advance by the Soviet Union beyond Afghanistan to be a direct threat to my country.

INTERVIEWER: With the Soviet invasion of Afghanistan, the Cold War took a turn markedly for the worse.

CARTER: Exactly. Well, we had been making good progress, I think, in alleviating the tension of the Cold War. I had explained my reasons for normalizing relations with China; we had concluded a very productive negotiation in Vienna for the SALT II treaty; we were having a very good response from the Soviet Union in permitting Jews to emigrate from their country because of our human rights policy, and I really felt that we were on the track to an alleviation of tension. And then Brezhnev made what I considered to be a very serious mistake, maybe because he was old and somewhat debilitated in his political strength, of invading Afghanistan. This was a major setback, and obviously, the Soviets had not tried to extend their effective . . . their hegemony beyond their borders since they had gone into Hungary and Czechoslovakia a generation earlier, so it was quite a change in their basic policy.

INTERVIEWER: I'd like to ask you briefly about the Horn of Africa. What view did you take of Soviet and Cuban activity in Ethiopia?

CARTER: I thought this was serious. When the Soviets moved into Ethiopia to assist the Communist dictator there, Haile Mariam Mengistu, I thought that this was a threat to the stability of Africa. And they denied that they were even involved, both the Soviets and the Cubans. We had adequate intelligence to intercept radio transmissions from Soviet troops and Cuban troops inside Ethiopia, to . . . I could even give them the names of the Soviet generals who were in Ethiopia, and we had messages, for instance, about a Soviet general whose wife was ill, and he had asked the Kremlin to let him go back home to visit his wife. When Gromyko came to the White House, and he and I were sitting across the table from each other, he denied, in looking me in the eye, that there were any Soviets in Ethiopia. And I said, "Mr. Foreign Minister, this is the information we have." He knew he was not telling me the truth, but it was the policy of the Soviet Union to claim they had no troops there. Somalia was trying to gain the area, I thought, from Ethiopia, so there was some equal responsibility on both sides for the war. I thought that Somalia should not be permitted to succeed in trying to take Ethiopian territory, and I refused to give the Somali government any weapons with which to fight the war. At the same time, I thought that the Soviets and the Cubans should get out of Ethiopia and let that be a domestic or local confrontation between two African countries and not see it expanded into a much wider hegemonic effort by the Soviets.

INTERVIEWER: Extremely clear answer—thank you very much. I'd like to end by asking you two general questions. What was your view of restricting the supply of oil, putting up the price of oil? What was your view of oil as a weapon?

CARTER: Well, there was . . . as is well known, the use of oil as a weapon was begun in 1973 when President Nixon was in office and I was governor of Georgia, and OPEC was formed, and oil was withheld . . . as an embargo weapon against any nation that had harmonious relations with Israel. So, the Arab embargo of oil created a very serious threat to our own nation's domestic well-being, or even our national security if you take it to extremes. So, when I became president four years later, the energy depletion and the excessive dependence of the United States on foreign oil was still a very pressing item on our nation's consciousness, including mine as the leader of my country. So, I began a very strong move for energy conservation, to reduce the waste of oil, and I raised fairly dramatically the ability to charge reasonable prices for oil instead of very low subsidized prices, with an excess profits tax so that the oil companies wouldn't benefit too much. This applied to oil and natural gas. So, I've always had an adverse reaction to the use of oil as a weapon. It's almost an act of war when it's done. One of the final items that was an obstacle to the peace treaty between Israel and Egypt was the fact that Israel was occupying Egyptian territory, including Egyptian oil wells, and it was this Egyptian oil that was being used to furnish Israel with an assured supply of petroleum products. And I had to work out at the last minute, with Begin, an agreement to return these oil wells to Egypt, and Egypt agreed through President Sadat to let Israel have first call on the oil produced in the Sinai region. And I also agreed with Israel that if Egypt should cut off the supply, that the United States would supply Israel with oil at the world market price. So, oil has always been a very difficult issue for us. Nowadays, the United States, many years later, has lowered its guard and we are not importing more than half our total oil consumed from foreign sources.

INTERVIEWER: Last question. What part did your Christian faith play in the formulation of your foreign policy and your fortitude in carrying it out?

CARTER: I don't think there's any doubt that my Christian faith has permeated my life in almost everything that I have done, as a businessman, as a family leader, as a governor and as a president. I happen to be a Baptist, with my father's own commitment to the total separation of church and state, in that the government cannot impose my religious beliefs on any other citizen of my country, and that my church shouldn't try to claim a privileged position in our secular society. But there's no doubt that my promise to tell the truth when I was in the White House, my commitment to basic human rights, the alleviation of suffering, the promotion of peace in Zimbabwe and in the Middle East, and my reticence to use military force to accomplish America's political goals are all compatible with my religious faith.

INTERVIEWER: Did prayer help you during Camp David, for example?

CARTER: Well, yes, there's no doubt that when I reached a crisis stage as president that prayer was always part of my conscious effort. At Camp David, for instance, the one time that I remember praying most fervently was when I got the word that Sadat was leaving Camp David and going back to Egypt, and he was through with the negotiations. So, I had on blue jeans and very casual clothes; I put on slightly more formal clothes and I went off in a corner and I said a silent prayer that when I went to Sadat's cabin, I might induce him to stay on for further peace talks. And of course, when I got to his cabin, I was ultimately successful. So, my prayers were always designed to let me act . . . I would say compatibly with God's will and in an honest way. I have been able to refrain from praying that I would be victorious in elections or that my favorite football team would win the championship and things of that kind.

INTERVIEWER: Mr. Carter, thank you very much indeed.

THE GOSPEL ACCORDING TO JIMMY

INTERVIEW BY WIL S. HYLTON
GQ
2005

WIL S. HYLTON: You call yourself a born-again evangelical Christian, but you draw the line at the word fundamentalist. Can you define those terms?

JIMMY CARTER: I define fundamentalism as a group of invariably male leaders who consider themselves superior to other believers. The fundamentalists believe they have a special relationship with God. Therefore, their beliefs are inherently correct, being those of God, and anyone who disagrees with them are, first of all wrong, and second inferior, and in extreme cases even subhuman. Also, fundamentalists don't relish any challenge to their positions. They believe any deviation from their own God-ordained truth is a derogation of their own responsibility. So, compromise or negotiating with others, or considering the opinion of others that might be different, is a violation of their faith. It makes a great exhibition of rigidity and superiority and exclusion.

It seems that the more devout a person becomes in their faith and their Bible and their church, the more difficult it would be not to feel that way. Paul established three little churches in Galatia on a supple but profound belief that we are saved by the grace of God through our faith in Jesus Christ. That was his basic message, and Peter and other disciples did

the same thing. What Paul condemned in the strongest letters is that believers in the little churches began to embellish
that fundamental with other requirements, saying that you
had to become a Jew first, you had to be circumcised to be a
Christian, you can't eat the meat that's been sacrificed to idols
and be a Christian, you have to worship on a particular holy
day to be a Christian, you have to accept a certain apostle as
the best representative of Christ to be a Christian. So, they
began to embellish the basic foundation of Christian faith
by human-created additional requirements. And that was the
origin of fundamentalism.

HYLTON: So, you would define fundamentalists as embellishers.

CARTER: Absolutely—and creating definitions of Christianity.
If you don't agree with my embellishment, then you can't be
one of us.

HYLTON: What about things that do seem to be in the
fundamentals, for example, I know you've grappled with
abortion.

CARTER: I've never believed that if Jesus was confronted
with the question, that he would approve abortion. There
are millions of people who disagree with me on both sides.
They believe that abortion begins when the male sperm is
ejaculated. Others believe that abortion is okay up until the
end of the first three months of the pregnancy. Others believe
that a woman should have full rights to control her own body.
I presume that those who believe in the different nuances

concerning abortion can all be faithful and devout Christians. I don't have any objection to that. But my own belief is that Christ would not approve abortion unless the woman's life was in danger.

HYLTON: If the problem with fundamentalists is that they impose their rules on others, you might also ask yourself, "What rules do *I* impose?" For example, you opposed federal funding of abortion.

CARTER: I did everything I possibly could to minimize abortion and to discourage abortion while still complying with the law as ordained by the Supreme Court.

HYLTON: But it seems like this is one of those areas where it's difficult to draw the line. You believe you know the will of God.

CARTER: If I were a purist in my faith, I couldn't hold public office and preside over a nation that honored abortion. But when I went into politics and I ran for office, I was willing as a state senator and as a governor and as a president to take an oath before God that I would uphold the laws of the districts that I served. There were times when I was able to change the laws. But until they were changed, I had to comply with them. So, when people have asked me about this, I always tell them that this was the most difficult issue I had to face, because I was inherently against abortion, but I was required to impose the law.

HYLTON: If you had the power to change that law, would you?

CARTER: I can live with *Roe v. Wade*. Late-term abortion is something I would have vetoed. I don't believe that late-term abortion is appropriate. That's obnoxious to me.

HYLTON: If abortion is against the will of God as you understand it, shouldn't you oppose it at the most elementary stage of development?

CARTER: Well, I have my personal beliefs, and in fact, my own personal belief is to do away with the death penalty as well. But our Constitution so far permits the states to be autonomous in imposing the death penalty, and the Supreme Court has gone back and forward on it. My wife and I interceded through the court as strong as we could a year ago, with public statements and letters to human rights organizations, to do away with the ruling that permitted the execution of juveniles. So, we have tried to intervene that way.

HYLTON: But not on abortion.

CARTER: That's correct.

HYLTON: You've also been able to blend your scientific background with your spiritual beliefs. Has it ever been difficult to reconcile the training of science, which demands evidence, with faith, which is in many ways the opposite?

CARTER: No. Faith is believing in something that cannot be proven. You can't prove the existence of God. You can't prove that Jesus Christ is the son of God. You can't prove many things in the Bible, so for someone to have confidence in that, you have to have faith.

HYLTON: Do you think that if you had been raised in an Islamic culture, you would be comfortable in that faith?

CARTER: I would surmise that I would.

HYLTON: But based on what you believe now, you would have been wrong.

CARTER: That may be true. But Jesus said, "Judge not, that you be not judged." It's not for me to say that an ignorant Ethiopian who lives around a lake at the origin of the Blue Nile, where I was four days ago, and has never heard of Christ is condemned. I can't believe that. And I can't say that a child as you just described, that grew up with Islamic teachings and that believes in Muhammad and Allah, would be condemned. It's not my role to condemn people. That's a role to be played by God Almighty.

HYLTON: But this would be about a sense of loss on your own part.

CARTER: There would be. To know what I know now, I would be aggrieved if I had never known about Jesus Christ, because I have tried to apply, in a faltering way, the teachings of Jesus Christ. It's been an inspiration to me, it's been a guide to me, it's been a stabilizing factor in my life. It has permeated my consciousness.

HYLTON: This will sound like the same question, but if you had been raised by atheists, do you think you would have had an inner feeling of faith?

CARTER: I think so.

HYLTON: Wouldn't it be hard without the guidance of others?

CARTER: I believe that when I approached adulthood, I would have been exploring the authenticity or the veracity, or the applicability of the Christian faith. If I had been raised as an atheist and I had gone into the outside world and all of a sudden, I realized that I was living in a nation where the majority of people profess faith in Christ, I would have wanted to explore the beliefs of others to see if it was applicable to me.

HYLTON: It seems difficult to imagine someone coming into the vast realm of religious offerings and having any idea where to begin. With so many options, they could very well all be wrong.

CARTER: I accept the fact that some of my beliefs could be wrong. There may be some fallibilities in my own personal beliefs, sure. I can't change my mind just because I think I might be wrong. My present beliefs have been evolved over seventy-five years of thought and study, analysis, teaching.

HYLTON: One of the other aspects of your life that struck me as a conflict between your experience and your scientific training was that you saw a UFO.

CARTER: I saw an unidentified flying object. I've never believed that it came from Mars. I know enough physics to know that you can't have vehicles that are tangible in nature flying from Mars, looking around, and then flying back. But I saw an object one night when I was preparing to give a speech to a Lions Club. There were about twenty-five of us men standing around. It was almost time for the Lions Club supper to start, which I would eat and then I would give a speech. I was in charge of fifty-six Lions Clubs in southwest Georgia back in the late sixties. And all of a sudden, one of the men looked up and said, "Look, over in the west!" And there was a bright light in the sky. We all saw it. And then the light, it got closer and closer to us. And then it stopped, I don't know how far away, but it stopped beyond the pine trees. And all of a sudden, it changed color to blue, and then it changed to red, then back to white. And we were trying to figure out what in the world it could be, and then it receded into the distance. I had a tape recorder—because as I met with members of Lions Clubs, I would dictate their names on the tapes so I could remember them—and I dictated my observations. And when I got home, I wrote them down. So that's an accurate description of what I saw. It was a flying object that was unidentified. But I have never thought that it was from outer space.

HYLTON: One of the promises you made in 1976 was that if you were elected, you would look into the reports from Roswell and see if there had been any coverups. Did you look into that?

CARTER: Well, in a way. I became more aware of what our intelligence services were doing. There was only one instance that I'll talk about now. We had a plane go down in the Central African Republic—a twin-engine plane, small plane. And we couldn't find it. And so, we oriented satellites that were going around the earth every ninety minutes to fly over that spot where we thought it might be and take photographs. We couldn't find it. So, the director of the CIA came and told me that he had contacted a woman in California that claimed to have supernatural capabilities. And she went in a trance, and she wrote down latitudes and longitudes, and we sent our satellite over that latitude and longitude, and there was the plane.

HYLTON: That must have been surreal for you. You're the president of the United States, and you're getting intelligence information from a woman in a trance in California.

CARTER: That's exactly right.

HYLTON: How did your scientific mind process that?

CARTER: With skepticism. Whether it was just a gross coincidence or . . . I don't know. But that's one thing that I couldn't explain. As far as covering up possible flights from distant satellites or distant heavenly bodies, I don't believe in that, and there's no evidence that it was ever covered up. Or extraterrestrial people coming to Earth, I don't think that's ever happened.

HYLTON: In a way, just the fact that you promised the American people you would look into it is reflective of how much of an outsider you were to Washington.

CARTER: That's true.

HYLTON: Looking back, do you think that you could have been elected if not for the hunger for honesty after Watergate?

CARTER: No, I don't think so. I didn't have any money, and I was almost completely unknown outside of Georgia, and I had never served in Washington. I had only spent a few days there in my entire life. But it was a propitious time for me. Fortune smiled on me. People were looking for some breath of fresh air, some outsider. I told the first ten people who I could get to come and hear me that if I ever made a misleading statement, they shouldn't vote for me. I said, "I'll never lie to you." And that resonated.

HYLTON: Once you got to Washington, even though you had a Democratic Congress, it wasn't easy.

CARTER: My main problem was with the liberal Democrats. I was conservative on defense. I had spent eleven years of my life in the Navy, and I wanted a strong defense. And I believed in a balanced budget. They thought that was anathema to the basic Democratic faith. After a few months, Ted Kennedy challenged me and told everybody to oppose what I was doing.

HYLTON: It sounds like there was a social component, too, with all the glad-handing that goes on in Washington and the drinks after tennis and things like that. You didn't like the politicking.

CARTER: That's true, and that was a mistake I made. I would have been better off if I had entwined myself into the social life of Washington with the *Washington Post* leaders and the evening cocktail party circuit. I would have made some alliances there that could have been quite valuable to me, but it was anathema to me. It was not my way of life. It was a political mistake.

HYLTON: It must have been a real slap in the face when Kennedy ran against you.

CARTER: Well, we've gotten over it now. He and I are basically compatible on overall political philosophy. So, I don't have any hard feelings. But when I got the nomination at the convention, Kennedy came on the stand and ostentatiously refused to shake hands with me. I went up and stuck out my hand; he stood there for a while and turned around. Wouldn't shake my hand. In front of six thousand or whatever it was Democratic delegates. And he never gave me any support.

HYLTON: Have you ever discussed that with Kennedy?

CARTER: We had one discussion in the White House as we were approaching the general election, but it was not a successful discussion. I tried to get Ted Kennedy to make a public endorsement of me and to urge his supporters to support me, but he was very, very cool. And never did do it. But that's beside the point. Of course, I hated to be defeated in 1980, but the way it's turned out, this has been by far the best time of my life.

HYLTON: Someone said that you were the only person in history who used the presidency as a stepping stone to greatness.

CARTER: I've heard that.

HYLTON: I wanted to talk briefly about the prospects in the Middle East. What are your feelings about the prospects for this Gaza pullout?

CARTER: Well, at the moment, I'm not hopeful. I have been recently, but I think now the prospects are not good because [Ariel] Sharon has announced that if any representatives of Hamas run for parliament, he is not going to permit the Palestinians to cross the checkpoints. There are hundreds of checkpoints, in some places every few hundred yards.

HYLTON: This has been one of the big issues with the Bush administration's policy in the Middle East, too: who to deal with and who not to deal with. I wonder if you could comment on the decision not to deal with [Yasser] Arafat.

CARTER: I think that was a mistake. They—Sharon and Bush together—castrated Arafat as far as any sort of political effectiveness. And then they condemned Arafat because he couldn't control the Palestinians. He was confined, as you know, to two or three rooms.

HYLTON: But the Bush administration points to that and says, "We may have lost four years, but we got Abu Mazen."

CARTER: Well, at this moment, I don't see any prospects for progress.

HYLTON: Probably your most famous speech was the "crisis of confidence" speech in 1979, and a critical element was the idea that we have to make sacrifices. Today we have a very different policy espoused, with Dick Cheney saying that conservation is a personal virtue and not a basis for policy. I wonder how you react.

CARTER: America is not at war. We're not really at war with terrorists. There is no commitment of the American people to make a sacrifice to deal with the threat of terrorism. We're not sacrificing our beliefs to accommodate those of France or Russia or others who might have participated in the Iraqi war.

And you can't find an American, except for a half of 1 percent who are in Iraq or who have loved ones in Iraq, who've made any sacrifice in the last three or four years. You haven't. I haven't. In fact, I make a lot of money, and my taxes have gone down. So, there's been a policy here that is incredible, of enriching people in a time of war and putting the burden on poor people and future generations in order to make sure we don't make sacrifices in order to meet the exigencies of threats to our country.

HYLTON: And whose failure is that?

CARTER: The leaders in Washington, from the White House to the majority in the House and Senate.

HYLTON: It's got to be hard for you as an ex-president, with the customary code of conduct that you're not supposed to be too critical. Is that a tough balancing act for you?

CARTER: Yes. Yes. There are some seminal changes that are being made in the basic policy of my country with which I disagree. There are some people that really believe that to remove taxation from the rich is the right way for this country to go. There are people who really believe that preemptive war is the right way for America to exert its foreign-policy influence. There are people who really believe that endangered species ought not to be protected because it might inhibit economic development. There are people who really believe that a minimum wage of half as much as it is in most developed countries is the right way for our country to be. But the American people have not yet decided which direction the country should go.

HYLTON: You feel like you can't afford, at this point, to be—

CARTER: Silent. Yes.

ON BEING DIAGNOSED WITH CANCER

CARTER CENTER PRESS CONFERENCE
AUGUST 20, 2015

JIMMY CARTER: Well, thank you all for coming this morning. I first want to give my special thanks to my wife, Rosalynn, who's busy talking right now, and to all the folks at the Carter Center, my Emory doctors, and literally hundreds of well-wishers who have called in or sent me letters or emails—and I've tried to answer as many of them as I could.

I think what I'll do this morning is just outline what's happened so far with my medical condition, and then toward the end, I'll give you a brief rundown of what I plan to do in the future, and then I'll answer some questions from the news media.

In May, I went down to Guyana to help monitor an election. I had a very bad cold, so I left there and came back to Emory so they could check me over. In the process, they did a complete physical examination, and the MRI showed that there was a cancer—well, a growth, a tumor, on my liver. And they did a PET scan, which kind of lights up a bad place, and it lit up, so they were pretty sure that there was a cancer before they operated on August 3 and removed it. The tumor was only about 2.5 cubic centimeters. They removed about 85 cubic centimeters, which is about a tenth of my liver, and they did a biopsy and found out it was indeed cancer, and it was melanoma. They had a very high suspicion then and now that the melanoma started somewhere else on my body and spread to the liver. The doctors tell me that about 98 percent of all the melanoma is skin cancer, and about 2 percent of melanomas are internal.

So then, I came back up here after that, and they did an MRI and found that there were four spots of melanoma on my brain. They are very small spots—about two millimeters, if you can envision what a millimeter is. I get my first radiation treatment for the melanoma in my brain this afternoon, and then I understand I'll have four treatments [with the drug pembrolizumab] scheduled at three-week intervals. (*The description of the treatment frequencies was edited to clarify the original remarks.*)

Yesterday they fitted me with a mask to hold my head perfectly still while the radiation goes into the right places, and I'm all prepared for that this afternoon. In addition, they have given me an IV with thirty minutes of pembrolizumab, which is a medicine used for melanoma that enhances the activity of the immune system.

Now, this is a medicine that's been approved in the United States. There are similar ones that have also been tested in Europe. My doctors will also continue to scan other parts of my body with MRI, a CAT scan, and PET scan to see where the melanoma originated; and so that will be an ongoing examination of my body for the next number of months, I presume, if it goes on that long.

Dr. Juan Sarmiento is the doctor at Emory that did the surgery on my liver. Dr. David Lawson is a specialist on melanoma. Dr. Curran, who's here, is a specialist on radiation treatment, and he's in charge of Winship Cancer Center. They're working very closely with other cancer centers around this nation—in particular, the MD Anderson Center in Houston, Texas, National Cancer Institute, Sloan Kettering, and others. I've had a lot of people call and recommend different places, and I referred those offers of help to the doctors, who have reached out to get acquiescence or approval of what they've decided to do in my treatment.

For a number of years, Rosalynn and I have planned on dramatically reducing our work at the Carter Center but haven't done it yet. We thought about this when I was eighty years old, and again when I was eighty-five. We thought about it again when I was ninety. And so, this is a propitious time, I think, for us finally to carry out our long-delayed plans; so, I'm going to cut back fairly dramatically on my obligations at Emory and at the Carter Center. As you know, the Carter Center has a full legal partnership with Emory. Half of our trustees are selected by Emory, and we approve them, and vice versa. The president of Emory University is on our board of trustees, as are Rosalynn and I, and we have built up a fairly substantial endowment to tide the Carter Center over when I'm not any longer able to raise funds, and we have now a little over $600 million in our endowment. But I'll continue to sign letters requesting contributions and make key calls to people who might be prospects, so I'll continue to help with the funding. The trustee meetings are held at the Carter Center, and I'll continue to attend those. And I'd like also to schedule the regular meetings with our fellows and directors, as they give detailed reports quite regularly on what we are doing with the fight against Guinea worm and with our peace programs and other health programs, and so forth. So, I'll continue to do that.

I can't really anticipate how I'll be feeling, obviously, but I'll have to defer quite substantially to my doctors in charge of the treatment. I understand that there will be the one radiation treatment and also four injections at three-week intervals, then they'll stop and take a look at what the results might have been, and I'll adhere to that schedule as much as possible. *(The description of the treatment frequencies was edited to clarify the original remarks.)*

The Carter Center is well prepared to continue without any handicap if Rosalynn and I do back away from a lot of the activities that we've been doing. The board of trustees decided last March that our grandson Jason Carter would take over as the chairman of the board, replacing Oz Nelson, which was Nelson's suggestion, to be effective at our meeting in November. So, Jason will be the chairman of the Carter Center's board of trustees, which is a body that makes the ultimate decisions about what projects the Center works on and budget matters and things of that kind. And then, of course, if he wants me to give him advice, I'll be delighted to do it, as I've done with some other people in the past. I was the chairman for a while, but I stepped down a number of years ago to give other people a chance to work on it.

So, I'll try as best I can to continue my work as a professor at Emory and to attend some of the meetings. But I would say that the rest of my plans will be to determine, by my consultations with the doctors, what I need to do to get adequate treatment for the melanoma that exists, at least has existed in my liver. They think they got it all there, but it has shown up now in four places in my brain, and it's likely to show up other places in my body as the scans detect it in the future.

So that's all I wanted to say to you, but I'll be glad to answer a couple questions if you have them.

REPORTER: Good morning, President Carter, Lori Geary with WSB-TV. I just want to get—what was your initial reaction, you know, when you heard that C word, the cancer word, and what doctors have said about your prognosis? You seem very optimistic; your spirits are very good.

CARTER: Well, at first, I felt that it was confined to my liver and that the operation had completely removed it, so I was quite relieved. And then, that same afternoon, an MRI of my head and neck showed up that it was already in four places in my brain. So, I would say that night and the next day, until I came back up to Emory, I just thought I had a few weeks left, but I was surprisingly at ease. You know, I've had a wonderful life, I've got thousands of friends, and I've had an exciting and adventurous and gratifying existence, so I was surprisingly at ease—much more so than my wife was. But now I feel, you know, that it's in the hands of God and my doctors, and I'll be prepared for anything that comes.

REPORTER: Thank you.

CARTER: Thank you.

REPORTER: Mr. President?

CARTER: Yes, hi.

REPORTER: Mr. President, you've just said that you expect that there will be further cancers diagnosed.

CARTER: Yes.

REPORTER: So, was it at all difficult—given the fact that you also just said that you thought maybe it was just a matter of a few weeks, was it difficult at all to decide to go ahead with treatment? I mean, does your faith play any role in the fact that you did that, or did you consider at any time not doing anything at all?

CARTER: No, I never have doubted that I would carry out the recommendations of Emory doctors. And so, when they said that they wanted to go ahead and find out other places that might show up cancer and treat them, I'm perfectly at ease with that—and I'm perfectly at ease with whatever comes. I do have a deep religious faith, which I'm very grateful for. And I was pleasantly surprised that I didn't go into an attitude of despair or anger or anything like that. I was just completely at ease, as Rosalynn would testify, I think, if you have any doubts about my veracity. But I've just been very grateful for that part of it, so I'm ready for anything, and looking forward to a new adventure.

REPORTER: President Carter, Katie Foody with the Associated Press. You just said that you felt at ease. Can you tell us a little bit more about your discussions with your doctors, with your family, and how you came to decide that you did want treatment and you wanted to pursue anything that your doctors did recommend would be appropriate for you?

CARTER: That never was a difficulty for me because I don't think I've ever deviated from a commitment to do what my doctors recommended, so that was not a big decision for me. I decided that to begin with. Dr. Curran is here, and I understand if you have any technical questions to ask him or medical questions, he'd be willing to answer any questions that you might have later on. But the three doctors have worked in close harmony with me. The surgeon who did the operation on my liver, Dr. Sarmiento, and Dr. Curran, who is a specialist on treatment of cancer, and also Dr. Lawson, who is a specialist on melanoma itself, have been like a team working very closely with me, and I have complete confidence in them.

They've been gracious enough to reach out to others who have volunteered to consult with them, and I understand they've shared even the MRI with some others. So, they're consulting, I guess, with the best cancer treaters in the world, and I'm very grateful that Emory is in charge.

REPORTER: Lynne Anderson with *The Atlanta Journal-Constitution*. First of all, President Carter, I'm so sorry and sad to hear this news. And I just have a basic question. How are you feeling?

CARTER: I feel good. I haven't felt any weakness or debility. The pain has been very slight. Right after the operation on my liver, I had a little bit of pain in my stomach. It was a laparoscopic operation. They made three very tiny incisions in my stomach. I had some pain in my right shoulder, strangely enough, but the doctor said that's expected as kind of a resonating pain that goes from your liver—internal organs up to your right shoulder if you have liver problems. And I think if you have a heart problem, it goes to your left shoulder, so—but I survived that. I only took the pain medicine for a few hours, and then I didn't have to take it anymore. I had a slight reaction last night to the first treatment of the pembrolizumab—a little bit of pain in my shoulder—and I went to bed about six o'clock and slept 'til eight o'clock this morning. I think that's probably the best night's sleep I've had in many years. So, I feel at ease, and I have been very lucky that the Emory doctors have been able to control any aspects of pain from the operation or from the presence of cancer.

REPORTER: Mr. President, Tom Jones from WSB-TV. You mentioned all the well-wishers. Has there been any one correspondence or call that really touched you?

CARTER: Well, both of the former presidents Bush called me at one time, and then George H. W. Bush, Bush Sr., called me again yesterday afternoon. I think I appreciated that very much, and their wives were there on the telephone with them. President Obama called; Vice President Biden called. Bill Clinton called, Hillary Clinton called, Secretary of State Kerry called—the first time they've called me in a long time. But I think the close friends that I've had around home that have done special things, to bring us, you know, peach pie and stuff like that, really made me feel emotional. My whole family—twenty-one other Carters that live in Georgia—they've all been down to see us. They'll be down again this weekend for my wife's birthday celebration. So I've just had a multiple effusion of gratitude.

REPORTER: Hi, Jonathan Karl with ABC News. Two questions. First, I saw a report that you told Habitat for Humanity that you would still like to go forward with your trip to Nepal in November. Do you still hope to make that trip?

CARTER: I still hope to go. It would require an airplane flight from Kathmandu to the Chitwan area, which is south, down towards the Indian border. And if I do that, I understand—I would have to talk to the doctors—but I understand from my schedule that it would require a five-week postponement of my last treatment, so that's what I'm going to have to consider. Up until this morning, I was completely committed to go to Nepal with Habitat for Humanity; but if I don't go, the rest of my family will probably go to take my place.

REPORTER: And if I can ask, you have really refined what it means to be a former president. Can you reflect on the work you have done since you left the White House and what you hope to still do?

CARTER: Well, the work of the Carter Center has been, I'd say, more personally gratifying to me, because when you're president, you have a responsibility for 350 million people, 3,000 members of the U.S. armed forces, budgets, and

Congress, and so forth. I was able to do a number of good things when I was president, for which I'm very grateful—that was the high point of my life, politically speaking. I would say that my having been president of the United States, a great country, has made it possible for me to have the influence and contact with people and knowledge that has been the foundation for the Carter Center.

But the Carter Center has a completely different approach. We deal with individual people in the smallest and most obscure and suffering villages—in the deserts and in the jungles of Africa. We've had programs in eighty different countries for the poorest and most destitute people in the world. And that has been, I'd say, far more gratifying personally, because we actually interact with families and with people who are going blind or who have lymphatic filariasis, which is elephantiasis, or who have Guinea worm and so forth. Going into the villages and learning about the people and what the actual needs are, then meeting those needs with a superb Carter Center medical staff, I think, has been one of the best things that ever happened to me. I've said several times that my life since the White House has been personally more gratifying, although the presidency was obviously the pinnacle of my political success, and also has laid the groundwork for my work at the Carter Center.

REPORTER: Do you still feel you have a lot of work left to do?

CARTER: Well, I do. And within the bounds of my physical and mental capability, I'll continue to do it. But I'm going to have to give the treatment regimen, I think, top priority.

REPORTER: Good morning, Mr. President. Hallie Jackson, NBC News. Given your current cancer diagnosis, given your family history with this disease, what message do you have to other cancer patients who are watching you go through this now?

CARTER: Well, I've read a lot about cancer, with the death of my father and my only brother and both my sisters from pancreatic cancer. For a long time, my family was the only one on earth that had as many as four people who died of pancreatic cancer—a very rare thing—though I think now they've found two or three other such families. After I left the White House and my brother and sisters continued to die, they did some special checks on my blood samples and some scans of different kinds. Pancreatic cancer does have some genetic cause—that's what I've read in some of the scientific documents—but it's exacerbated by smoking cigarettes, which I've never done, and so the melanoma is a completely different thing. And it may be that in the future the melanoma would show up on my pancreas, but they have not found that to be true in the last few weeks. Generally, they watch the pancreas quite closely, and so far, the only place they've known about the cancer has been in my liver and my brain. I would say that one of the greatest scientific developments in the last five years has been with two kinds of cancer. One is lung cancer and the other one is melanoma. In addition to radiation and chemotherapy, the treatment for melanoma has included the use of these medicines that enhance the function of the self-regulating aspect of the immune system—they make your immune system more active—and so that's a basic approach, and there are several of these medicines.

REPORTER: So, the message to other patients? Is your message one of hope, is it acceptance?

CARTER: It's one of hope and acceptance, yes—hope for the best and accept what comes, you know. I think I have been as blessed as any human being in the world, having become the president of the United States of America and governor of Georgia, the work at the Carter Center, a big and growing family, thousands of friends, and living to—I'll be ninety-one years old the first of October—everything has been a blessing for me, so I'm thankful and hopeful.

REPORTER: President Carter, Kane Farabaugh with Voice of America.

CARTER: Hi, Kane.

REPORTER: I wanted to ask, what has been—you said that you've sort of taken a pragmatic approach to the treatment and to the news—but what has been the most difficult part about the news for you in the past couple of weeks?

CARTER: Well, I haven't had any difficult treatment aspect yet. You know, the liver surgery was fairly extensive. They removed about one-tenth of my liver, I understand. But it healed up quickly, and I had minimal pain. I had the first of the four drug treatments yesterday, to be followed this afternoon by the radiation treatment, and then by the remaining immunotherapy treatments every three weeks, and then it will recess. So, I haven't had any unpleasantness yet.

(The description of the treatment frequencies was edited to clarify the original remarks.)

REPORTER: Is it difficult to step away from all of the busy activities?

CARTER: That's a bad part. I really wanted to go to Nepal to build houses. This would have been our thirty-third year of going without fail, and I was very hopeful about that. But if it interrupts the treatment regimen, then I think I need to get the treatment.

REPORTER: Hello, President Carter. Karyn Greer, CBS46 News, and just wondering. You touched upon it a little bit. In your illustrious career, as you said—governor here, president, even as husband, father, grandfather—share with us what you're most proud of and if there's anything you might have done differently or thought maybe, "I wish I had not done that"?

CARTER: Well, the best thing I ever did was marry Rosalynn. That's the pinnacle of my life, and we've had sixty-nine years together—still together—and so that's the best thing that happened to me. But I think getting involved in politics and going up, you know, as a state senator, then a governor, and then president of the United States is obviously a glorious event. And we have a growing family. We have twenty-two grandchildren and great-grandchildren—twelve grandchildren and ten great-grandchildren now, and they're coming every year—so we have a good and harmonious family. And I would say the haven for our lives has been in

Plains, Georgia. I plan to teach Sunday school this Sunday and every Sunday—as long as I'm, you know, physically and mentally able—in my little church. We have hundreds of visitors who come to see the curiosity of a politician teaching the Bible, so I continue that. I've just had a lot of blessings.

REPORTER: And anything you wish, I'm sorry, that you had not done or that you'd done differently?

CARTER: I wish I'd sent one more helicopter to get the hostages, and we would have rescued them, and I would have been reelected. But that may have interfered with the foundation of the Carter Center. And if I had to choose between four more years and the Carter Center, I think I would choose the Carter Center. It could have been both.

REPORTER: President Carter, Donna Lowry with 11Alive, WXIA-TV. I wonder—you just talked about your big family. And with this diagnosis, have you encouraged them to see the doctor? Are you seeing that there's more interest in finding out what's going on with each one of them?

CARTER: Yeah, I don't think there's any doubt that my descendants have some genetic challenge from the pancreatic cancer and my melanoma, so whatever their doctors recommend for blood tests or things like that as a precautionary measure for the other family members, I think that would probably be put into effect. But I haven't discussed that with them, and I don't know the answer yet.

I can get two or three more questions. Go ahead.

REPORTER: President Carter, Greg Bluestein with *The Atlanta Journal-Constitution*. I wonder, how did you break the news to your family?

CARTER: Well, I found out toward the end of May that I had a spot on my liver that was suspect, and I think I put in my diary that I didn't tell Rosalynn until about the fifteenth of June. And then, when I found out that I definitely had cancer, my key members of my family came into the Carter Center, and I gave them a briefing and our chief executive officer a briefing about what the prospects were. I put out a statement to the public about the first surgery and another one when we found out that it had metastasized, and then we called this press conference. I didn't say what kind it was, didn't say it was melanoma. I didn't say it had spread to my brain; I just said to other parts of my body. So as quickly as I could, I've told the public and my family the things about which I was absolutely certain, rather than just guessing what might happen. *(This section was edited slightly to clarify the sequence of press statements.)*

REPORTER: President Carter, thank you. Sanjay Gupta with CNN.

CARTER: Yeah, I know.

[*Laughter*]

CARTER: I've been taking all these other questions so I could get to you, Sanjay.

REPORTER: I have a couple of questions, a little bit more specific, about the medical aspects. You became ill, you said, in May and came back early to the United States.

CARTER: Yeah.

REPORTER: They had an MRI at that time that showed this liver mass. But it wasn't until two months later, my understanding from your comments, that you had the operation.

CARTER: That's right.

REPORTER: I'm wondering about that time period. Was there a consideration not to do anything during that time period?

CARTER: No.

REPORTER: And also, just quickly, the medications, you said you're following the recommendations of your doctor. Were you given options, and how did you weigh those options?

CARTER: I was given a complete rundown on the options that were available. And when they made a recommendation on a particular kind of medical treatment—I had the IV yesterday—I took their advice. And we knew, I would say the end of June, that I had to have an operation on my liver, but I had an extensive book tour scheduled in fourteen or fifteen cities, and I wanted to do that. The doctors told me that it was a very slow-growing cancer, apparently. They said it wouldn't make a difference between the middle of July and the third day of August, so we scheduled it when I got through with the book tour. Coincidentally, and not more importantly, my surgeon had scheduled a vacation trip in Spain. And so, the combination of all those things just caused me to wait until everything was ready. I stayed very busy during that time, and I didn't tell anybody much about it, except Rosalynn.

REPORTER: Thank you.

CARTER: Did you have another question, Sanjay?

REPORTER: No, that's it.

CARTER: Okay, thank you.

REPORTER: President, Wright Gazaway at WALB in Albany. You mentioned Plains there. Talk a little bit about the support of them and what that's meant to you.

CARTER: Well, Plains is my home. You know, I was born there, my wife was born there, and I knew Rosalynn when she was first born. I was three years older, and still am. And Plains has always been a haven for us. When I got out of the Navy in 1953, I came back to Plains, and I was a farmer for about seventeen years. And then, when I got through being governor, I came back to Plains. When I got through with being president, I came back to Plains. And now, no matter where we are in the world, we're always looking forward to getting back home to Plains. That's where our land is. We've had the same farm since 1833. We have a newer farm we got in 1904. We still grow peanuts, cotton, and corn on the farm. And so, my roots are there, and my closest friends are there—and our little church is there, which is very important to me. So, Plains has just been the focal point of our life. And a good many visitors come there every year—about eighty thousand, I think, on an official count—to find out how a president could have come from this little tiny town. They learn about my schooling and things of that kind. So, Plains means a lot to me. Okay. Let's not add anybody else to the line.

REPORTER: Thank you. President Carter, Jesus Cateri with *Mundo Hispanico* newspaper. I wonder if you have discussed with your family or closest—your call—how do you see this organization in the future, the Carter Center?

CARTER: How do I feel—what?

REPORTER: How do you see the Carter Center in the future? Have you discussed that?

CARTER: Well, I think the Carter Center's future will be equal to what it's been in the past. It's been expanding every year as far as the number of people we treat for terrible diseases and things of that kind. I understand that this coming year we'll treat 71 million people on Earth for diseases so that they won't have the afflictions that they've had throughout their lifetimes. We've finished one hundred troubled elections to bring democracy and freedom to people, and we still try to bring peace. So, we've concentrated on peace and human rights and democracy and freedom and the alleviation of suffering, and I would say that in every one of those areas, the Carter Center's overall function and plans for the future are still expanding. And I'm completely confident that those plans can be realized without my everyday, you know, constant involvement in different projects. And I'll still be coming to the trustees' meeting as long as I'm able and meeting with our directors and others who carry out the programs.

REPORTER: And have you received messages from Latin America, where the Carter Center has participation?

CARTER: Well, I've had a lot of messages the last few days from Latin America. I'll be meeting next week, soon—I don't know if it's next week, but in the next month—with a group from Panama, and I've already approved that program on my schedule. We've maintained a wide range of programs in Latin America, primarily to try to do away with conflicts within the country, including between the news media and the executive branch of government when they try to stamp out freedom of the press, and also to foment peaceful relationships. We still have an ongoing program in six countries in Latin America— just about finished—to do away with onchocerciasis or river blindness. We still have just a small cluster of people, the Yanomami people—about twenty-five thousand, I think, total population on the border between Venezuela and Brazil— we're going to continue to work on that. So, we'll continue to work in Latin America.

REPORTER: Good morning, Mr. President. I'm Scott Kimbler, News Radio 106.7 here in Atlanta. As Jason is preparing to take over as chairman of the board of the Carter Center, you have very much been the face of peace negotiations since the time that you left office. As he is continuing the efforts in the health and humanitarian efforts of the Carter Center, will he also be active, and will you be advising him in future international conflicts that the Carter Center may be asked to negotiate?

CARTER: Well, the chairman of the board of trustees and the entire body of trustees—about twenty-three, I think—make the final decisions. They make the ultimate choices of what we do and how much money we spend and how many people we send out and that sort of thing, and so the chairman of the board is very deeply involved in making those ultimate decisions and presenting them to the board of trustees. So, I presume that, as Oz Nelson has done in the last few years superbly, the new chairman, Jason, will use the best experience that he can derive for all the programs of the Carter Center. He may not be directly involved in as many direct peace negotiations and so forth as I. But he'll be going, for instance, to Myanmar for the election the first part of November, and he'll be heading up the Carter Center delegation to monitor that very important election.

REPORTER: Maria Saporta, longtime journalist in Atlanta, the *Saporta Report*, and now the *Atlanta Business Chronicle*.

CARTER: I know.

REPORTER: You have had such a scope of work in your life. In the time that you have left, what would give you the most satisfaction to see something happen—peace in the Middle East or eradication of polio? What are those things that you would hold onto the most that would give you the greatest satisfaction for the world if you can look at the state of the world and how you've been working in efforts to try and keep peace?

CARTER: Well, in international affairs, I would say peace for Israel and its neighbors. That's been a top priority of mine— in foreign-policy projects—for the last thirty years. Right now, I think the prospects are more dismal than anytime I remember in the last fifty years. The whole process is practically dormant. The government of Israel has no desire for a two-state solution, which is the policy of all the other nations in the world, and the United States has practically no influence compared to past years in either Israel or Palestine. So, I feel very discouraged about it, but that would be my number one foreign-policy hope. As far as the Carter Center is concerned, I would like to see Guinea worm completely eradicated before I die—I'd like the last Guinea worm to die before I do. I think right now, we have eleven cases. We started out with 3.6 million cases. I think we have two cases in South Sudan, one case in Ethiopia, one case in Mali, and seven cases in Chad. That's all the Guinea worms in the world, and we know where all of them are, so obviously that would be my top priority.

MODERATOR: This will be our last question.

REPORTER: Good morning, President Carter. Christopher King with CBS46 News here in Atlanta. You've fought many political battles throughout your career. How tough do you expect this fight against cancer will be?

CARTER: Well, it will be tough on my part. You know, I'm an acquiescent and cooperating patient. Within the bounds of my own judgment, I'll do what the doctors recommend for me to extend my life as much as possible. So, I don't look on this as any hardship on me. They have means, they say— and I trust them completely—to alleviate the aftereffects or side effects of the different treatments. They've had a lot of treatments ongoing with different patients, thousands of them in the world, and so I don't anticipate any troubling pain or suffering or deprivation on my part.

REPORTER: Thank you, Mr. President.

CARTER: Thank you all very much for coming. I appreciate it. I don't know if we—Dr. Curran, do you want to add anything or . . .? If you have any particular questions, Dr. Curran can correct my mistakes.

Okay, I'm leaving. Thank you all very much.

ON CIVIL RIGHTS AND JUSTICE

INTERVIEW BY DERRECK KAYONGO
C-SPAN
MAY 20, 2016

C-SPAN: Now, the first in a series of National Archives Conversations on Rights and Justice, which kicked off at the Jimmy Carter Presidential Library and Museum in Atlanta in May. Here's a conversation with President Jimmy Carter and Derreck Kayongo, a former Ugandan War refugee, who's now the CEO of the National Civil and Human Rights Center.

DERRECK KAYONGO: Good afternoon, everyone. Welcome to a lovely day. I want you to specifically thank President Carter for giving us this wonderful opportunity, and he's healthy. Look at him.

JIMMY CARTER: But I'm not as well-dressed as you are.

KAYONGO: We'll talk about that in a bit. My name is Derreck Kayongo and I'm the CEO for the Center for Civil and Human Rights, and I'm very proud to be here. We're going to do a couple of things. We're going to do some quick housekeeping. Please take off your cell phones if you have one into vibrate, I think is what they call it these days. When we are done with the program, if you could still wait a little bit for me and the president to walk out, that would be lovely as well. Then we'll have some Q and A after our little discussion.

So, if you have any questions, write them down and pass them along and we'll have them answered. President Carter, we are so delighted to talk to you today, but there's a lot of things going on as you can imagine.

CARTER: I've heard about it. Yeah.

KAYONGO: Today's conversation is around rights and justice. It's a national conversation that is really, really serious, 'cause we see a lot on TV right now, and particularly around the Bill of Rights, which some of them include the Fourteenth Amendment, which is civil rights. I was curious to see and hear from you what you think about civil rights today versus yesterday.

CARTER: Well, recently I've been reading about the Founding Fathers. I've read a book about James Madison and Jefferson and Washington later, just to see again after many years of study, a long time ago, about those early days of our own country. As you all may know, the first draft of the Constitution did not include the Bill of Rights, but they couldn't get enough states to ratify the Constitution of the United States until the Bill of Rights were added, and so that was a very major undertaking. James Madison and others helped to draft those, those finally accepted ten amendments to the Constitution known as the Bill of Rights. That did not include everyone. It wasn't until after the Civil War when the Thirteenth, Fourteenth, and Fifteenth Amendments were passed, and then let me ask you all, when did the women get a right to vote in this country?

AUDIENCE: 1920.

CARTER: That's not right. That's when white women got the right to vote.

AUDIENCE: That's right.

CARTER: That's a very important thing to remember because in 1920, the Constitution was passed, but when they were said that women had a right to vote, well, you couldn't discriminate because of sex, it just really included white women. It wasn't until thirty-something years later that the civil rights laws were passed when Lyndon Johnson was president after the civil rights movement, and African American women also got the right to vote. So that was an important issue. Then the Twenty-fourth Amendment came along later, and you didn't have to pay poll tax, but until then in the South, in some southern states, you had to pay a poll tax in order to vote. So, you see that it's been a step-by-step progressive element. I would say in the sixties and seventies, the United States breathed a sigh of relief because Harry Truman, when I was on the submarine, ordained in 1948 that there would be no discrimination in the military forces or in the civil service. Then that was about seven years before Rosa Parks sat in the front of a bus or before Martin Luther King Jr., became famous as a leader of the civil rights movement.

Then of course, as I mentioned earlier, when that was successful, then, of course, we basically passed the Civil Rights Act and people all over the country could vote. I and most other leaders in our country said, "Well, we've finally succeeded. We've finally provided for equality of treatment for all of our people." That was a fairly brief period of relaxation and self-satisfaction and self-congratulations. But we've seen lately, particularly with the abuse of mostly white policemen against African Americans and so forth, that we still have a long way to go, so I would say that we've had a relapse. Nowadays, there seems to be another stirring of a deeper commitment by our country to take another look at ourselves and see what can be done about the rights for everyone. This includes the gays and lesbians and so forth, as well as people with different races. So, we're in a constant struggle in the United States of America to provide, I'd say, a beacon light for other nations to follow and for ourselves to benefit as well. So, it's been a long continuing struggle that still goes on.

KAYONGO: At the Center for Civil and Human Rights, right now, we are looking at turning that into a voting precinct.

CARTER: Yes.

KAYONGO: I have an interesting story around that. When I worked for you as an election monitor—

CARTER: Yes.

KAYONGO: —when I was at Emerson, went to Ethiopia to help them vote.

CARTER: I remember those days. Yes.

KAYONGO: Yeah, and then Sierra Leone, we went together. I had never voted before.

CARTER: Ah.

KAYONGO: I'm Ugandan, and I had never had a chance to vote in my own country. I tell the story that I got the chance to vote for the first time in the United States, and I woke up at three in the morning. I was like the South Africans; I was in line. But the idea of an African young boy to come into this country and be afforded the same justices that regular born citizens were afforded was remarkable. So, now that we have this issue of voting going on, how do you feel about it? It's a big election year.

CARTER: Yeah. We've had a large number of people turn out to vote this year. Some new voters for, I'd say Trump and Bernie Sanders, that hadn't voted before in both parties. But unfortunately, I would say within the Republican Party, particularly state by state, as they have become ascendant or domineering in the state legislature and in the governor's offices, they have tightened up the ability to vote by requiring complicated acquisition of an ID card. So, this has discriminated against many people who are very poor, who've never had a driver's license, I'd say older people who are in nursing homes that don't have a need to drive their own automobiles. So, I think we still see a very deliberate move on the part of some people to exclude those that are not likely to vote for them. When I was governor of Georgia, there was a pretty wide move throughout the country to increase the number of people who voted.

So, in Georgia, we passed a law that was very interesting, and we designated every high school principal in Georgia to be a voting registrar. Every high school had a voting registrar as the head of a student body. Every May or so, I would have a contest in Georgia that, while I was governor, to see which high school could register the most new people to vote who just were approaching the age of eighteen. When I got to the White House and attempted to do the same thing, I found that it was impossible. Tip O'Neill, who was, I'd say a liberal Democrat, finally came to me one day and said, "Mr. President, you are not going to be successful with this because neither Democrats nor Republicans want to open up the rights to vote to a lot of new voters because they're in office because the presently qualified voters have put them there and they don't want a whole bunch of new, incomprehensible, unpredictable voters to come in and vote."

So, it's a bipartisan reluctance to let voting be open and free and universal. For a long time, the Carter Center monitored all the elections in China and there were a lot of them. We were restricted to the 650,000 small villages, which are now part of the Communist Party system. And in China, in those little villages, everyone is automatically registered to vote when they reach the age of eighteen, which I think we should have in this country as well. Men and women and so forth, you don't have to be a member of the Communist Party. So, that's the kind of thing that we need to do in this country, is to let there be universal voting without going through any procedure once you reach the age to vote.

KAYONGO: So, that's part of the civil rights kind of issue. We have then human rights, which are facing an affront around the world.

CARTER: That's true.

KAYONGO: I think what is really particularly perturbing is this idea that people feel that rights around the world are being denied, and you are involved heavily in the subject matter. So—

CARTER: The Carter Center is, yes.

KAYONGO: —from the Middle East, from Southern Africa, and all these others, what do you think about when you think about human rights today versus yesterday?

CARTER: That's been a very disappointing thing. I'm not just being critical today, but I think the best thing to do is to point out opportunities for improvement rather than just bragging on what we've done. We had an era when I was in the Navy of reaching for greatness in moral and ethical values as human beings. It's only happened once in history so far as I know, and that was immediately after the Second World War when perhaps 80 million people were killed. In 1945, in San Francisco, we assembled about forty-five nations or so, the ones that were victorious in the war primarily, and they established the United Nations with the idea of peace, peace. And the United Nations and the Security Council were designed so that it would prevent wars in the future. A few years later, the Universal Declaration of Human Rights was passed and adopted with some caveats.

The South Africans wouldn't agree for Blacks to vote. Russia would not permit free leaving [of] Russia and so forth, so there were a few caveats, but most of the time people voted [for] the Universal Declaration of Human Rights. I would say, at that moment, human beings looked at the combined commitment of the great religions—Christianity, Judaism, Islam, Buddhism, and so forth, and Hinduism—and they took the finest elements of every one of those great religions and put them down into thirty brief paragraphs that comprised the Universal Declaration of Human Rights. And that was almost a perfect picture of how everybody should be treated equally, with equal rights. So, the United Nations Security Council has abandoned its commitment to peace. If you are a powerful nation with a permanent member and you have a right to veto, you can do almost anything, and the Security Council will not condemn you.

I think the United States has sent armed troops to about thirty countries to fight under the general approbation or approval of the United Nations since the Second World War. Other countries can do the same thing if they're powerful enough. I wrote an op-ed piece for the *New York Times* a few years ago, two years ago. It showed that the United States is now violating at least ten of the thirty paragraphs in the Universal Declaration of Human Rights. A lot of those relate to the discrimination against women who are supposed to be equal. It's not just Blacks being equal to whites and so forth, so I think we have a long way to go still.

We need to reassess the basic purpose of the United

Nations to be for peace, not armed conflict, to resolve issues and recommit ourselves to the basic principles of human rights. I would urge all of you to just call up on Google, Universal Declaration of Human Rights, and you'd see it, you can read it in a couple of minutes. There's thirty paragraphs, and it's spelled out what you should do on human rights, and it's easily violated and it's easily justified, particularly after something like 9/11, the United States clamped down and took away our own civil rights, including some of mine. That's true as far as freedom of knowing information of your own. So, we have a long way to go.

KAYONGO: There's an interesting lady in the audience here today, Mrs. Abernathy.

CARTER: Yeah.

KAYONGO: She and I were talking over lunch, and she was recounting her husband's work and everybody's work in the civil rights movement. I was thinking how that connects to the human rights movement.

CARTER: Yeah.

KAYONGO: Do you as a Georgian feel proud of what the state has gone through and has worked through the civil rights movement? Because you're apparently the home of the civil rights movement. Am I right?

CARTER: Yes, pretty much.

KAYONGO: Yeah.

CARTER: Well, Martin Luther King Jr., is from Georgia, and we are very proud of what he did, and his family did, and the people associated with him. But there was a time during the fifties when Georgia was very negative on the civil rights movement, and we condemned Martin Luther King Jr., as a Communist and somebody that was trying to overthrow or change the basic structure of a federal government, of a U.S. government. For a hundred years, we had legal discrimination against Black people from 1865, you might say, almost to 1965. It was a combined commitment of churches and the U.S. Congress, and the U.S. Supreme Court and the American Bar Association, all said it's okay to discriminate against African Americans and to consider whites are superior. So, that was a major accomplishment for him and for those heroes who were in the civil rights movement.

Georgia was one of the few southern states that didn't oppose the change in integrating our schools, for instance, after the Supreme Court ruled that they should be no longer separate but equal. Other states had leaders in Arkansas and so forth that stood in the schoolhouse door, and in some cases, the U.S. had to send armed troops down to make them comply. So, we've had a good chance in this state to do well. Of course, recently with the LGBT, that was passed by the legislature and the governor very wisely vetoed that legislation. So, we're distinguished now against North Carolina, who in the past has been quite enlightened on civil rights, but it shows that we have another battle to fight after the race issue is, we hope someday will be resolved. Equally, I think we have the challenge of dealing with gay people and lesbians and transgender people.

KAYONGO: Two more questions before we go to the audience, does this need by youth today to be part of the petitioning for rights—

CARTER: Yeah.

KAYONGO: —you see that in the Black Lives Matter expression, and you see that in the kids in Africa who are speaking out. You see Brazil is having a rough time, Argentina, everybody is having a rough time. How do the youth today take this mantle of rights, and do it in a way that is respectable and also influential?

CARTER: If the young people don't do it, it won't be done. It's the young people's say, let's just take for instance, college age, whether you're in college or not, that's a time in a human being's formative years when they have a maximum degree of considering new ideas, from their classmates, from their professors, from reading more extensively than they have in the past. They also are unbound by preserving the status quo. Almost as soon as you graduate from college, you lose a substantial part of your human freedom. If you get a job with Delta Air Lines or Coca-Cola company or a bank, or if you get a job teaching school, you have to comply with the policies of your corporation or the school system.

You leave that and you lose that freedom that you had on the college campus to speak out with a single voice or get four or five people to join you or maybe forty or fifty to join you, so that's when there's a stirring of self-analysis, I would say maybe conscience, and you say, "What can I do to improve this world?" But that is very quickly stamped out when you get a job or when you start having to support a family, whether you're a boy or girl, a man or woman. So, I think that that's why that in almost every country on earth, it's the young people who have started the revolutions that have brought about changes or improvements in society.

KAYONGO: Do you think today in the United States we are doing a good job bringing up kids that understand moral aptitude?

CARTER: I think so. I believe on most college campuses, just for instance, and I'm including their peer groups who might not be in college, there is an effort by, in most college campuses, not all of them, to originate new ideas and new concepts and to encourage the students to adopt higher ideals or higher aspirations of moral values and ethical values and to question the political arrangement or the societal arrangements in which they were grown up. As I said earlier, when you get to be older than they are and start having a family of your own, you don't want to rock the boat. You don't want to endanger your own job. You don't want to become unemployed when you have a wife or children to take care of and so forth. So, I would say that in the United States now we have an adequate degree of stirring opportunities on the campus to speak out in an innovative or sometimes even a semi-revolutionary way. Yeah.

KAYONGO: Those of you have questions, please. Oh, there's one out there. I don't see very well, but yes.

AUDIENCE MEMBER: As the leader of the administration that set up a separate department of education, and congratulations on that, do you think we would benefit and would you favor mandatory courses in the curriculum, perhaps as early as elementary school, on human and civil rights, conflict resolution and negotiation?

CARTER: That's a hard question for me to answer because I think when you start having the federal government, I presume you would say, to mandate that you have to have this or that course for fourth graders or eighth graders or seniors in high school, that interferes with the basic commitment I have to let local people decide on their own curriculum. But I would say that there should be within every school a basic social science class showing the history of human rights, which we've just covered in a few minutes in this forum, and also encourage the students to learn about what their own country is doing. Yes, I think it'd be a good idea, but I think you have to be careful not to intrude too much on the local board of education's right to set their own curriculum.

AUDIENCE MEMBER: Mr. President, thank you for being here today.

CARTER: Sure.

AUDIENCE MEMBER: You have lived a long and full life

and the world has changed so much in your lifetime. We're looking in the past and the archives, but we're also looking in the future. What tenets or what flavor should we look at the future to stage the debate as we deal with this changing world we live in today?

CARTER: Well, I grew up during the Great Depression years on a farm. All my neighbors were African American, and all my playmates were Black. The ones with whom I worked in the field were Black. Until I was a teenager, I never realized that they had mandatorily separate and unequal schools. I never realized that their parents couldn't vote. I never realized that my playmates' parents couldn't serve on the jury, that they were deprived of basic rights. So, it was a time for me to learn all about that. I believe that we have an obligation now as adults to make sure that our children understand not only the highest ideals of what a society should be to provide equal opportunity, equal rights to everyone, but also to look at the history of successes in the past and to glorify the champions like Andy Young and Martin Luther King Jr., Rosa Parks and others that I need not mention.

AUDIENCE MEMBER: Who are your political heroes?

CARTER: Well, I'd say Lyndon Johnson and Harry Truman. I had boycotts operate against my business, but I never did have a threat to my life and so forth like others have had. So, but, anyway, to teach the history of what has been done in the past and we could all just, within our own families, we can exalt those who were so heroic and far thinking in the past and brought about changes, but also to point out that their achievements have not been perpetuated because of a natural tendency of every one of us to feel superior to somebody else.

We all have an element of pride ingrained within us that I'm at least better than somebody else. I'm at least better than a drug addict or at least better than an alcoholic. I'm at least better than a prisoner. I'm at least better than maybe a Black person. I'm at least better than a woman. We have those misconceptions that at least we are better than somebody else, but we need to guard them against that. But I think that can be done obviously within a home better and also to some degree, as the gentleman suggested here, in the school climate.

KAYONGO: There are yellow cards in your program, so we will have people collect those so we can grab these questions and get them on the air. We are webcasting, and so we have people who are tweeting, who are sending questions as well at different schools. So, there are volunteers coming around to collect these and we will bring them to you to read so that they can get on—

CARTER: But I've got to go to a Willie Nelson concert tonight.

KAYONGO: Wow. I hope I can come. While we wait for the collection of questions and some of the things, one of the biggest things that is interesting right now is the subject matter around religion.

CARTER: Yes.

KAYONGO: I think that some people now are either happy or sad that the new mayor of London happens to be a Muslim.

CARTER: I spent last weekend in London, and so I was able to join in the celebration of most people that he was elected.

KAYONGO: How do you think that is different from us and their passions around this particular person?

CARTER: Well, this young man, who is quite highly qualified, and I don't think anybody doubted about it. He won without any equivocation. He won a clear victory, although, he is a Muslim. London society just from observing people in the parks and on the streets is quite diverse now and becoming more so. But I think with the present quandary in which Europe finds itself closing its doors to refugees because many of them happen to be Islamic and that faith, I think this has been a clear signal for all of Europe to observe. So, I'm very pleased with that.

KAYONGO: In fact, most people don't know that in our Congress we do have a congressman who happens to be Muslim, and one who happens to be Buddhist who happens to be in this room today. But here's a question for you from the audience. "How do we impress upon [the] younger generation, first time eligible voters, that change has actually occurred even though we have more work to do? How do we restore hope?"

CARTER: Well, it's hard to answer that question, how do we convince the young people? But in our schools and our family life, which I mentioned earlier, we can certainly outline the history of the struggle for human rights because a lot of people think that the human rights that we presently enjoy have always been with us, particularly in the United States of America. We don't realize that for many years women could not vote and Black women could not vote till much later and that people who didn't pay poll taxes could not vote, we don't realize, even our original constitution didn't have any bill of rights in it. So, I think the first segment of our session here is a quick history that we ought to share with our young people.

KAYONGO: This is an interesting one. It's around the idea of power and is absolute power corrupt. Absolutely.

CARTER: Yeah.

KAYONGO: "Is power corrupt inherently?" is the first question.

CARTER: Is what?

KAYONGO: Power corrupt inherently. This current election season has, in my opinion, in the person's opinion, shown that there's no need for Super PACs.

CARTER: No need for Super PACs?

KAYONGO: Yeah.

CARTER: Like was ordained by the Supreme Court, with Citizens United?

KAYONGO: Yeah, I think they're talking about the ones that go behind your back when you're campaigning and they—

CARTER: I think one of the stupidest decisions that the Supreme Court has ever made was Citizens United, where they ordained that a corporation had the same characteristics under the Constitution as a human being. Now we have massive infusions of money into the political campaigns. When I ran for office, it was completely different. We raised money just a few dollars at a time, and there was a limit on what anybody could contribute. When I ran in the general election against Gerald Ford, who was an incumbent president, and later against the challenger, Ronald Reagan, you know how much money I raised for the general election? Zero.

KAYONGO: Zero?

CARTER: I didn't have to raise any money. We accepted the one dollar per person that a taxpayer can indicate on his tax return form.

KAYONGO: Wow.

CARTER: You can check a little check, you have to do it yourself, and that puts a dollar in the pot. So, Gerald Ford and I shared the money that was in that pot. We didn't ask a single contributor to give us money. Now we have what I would call legal bribery in this country because every candidate for Congress, for governor, for U.S. senator, for president, has to go out to people and ask for money. You can't be considered to be a nominee for president unless you can raise one or two hundred thousand or even more. So, I think that has deteriorated our own electoral system in this country far below the standards that the Carter Center requires when we monitor elections. We wouldn't dream of monitoring an election in a country that had the same rules that the United States has.

We've done more than a hundred troubled elections and we require that they have a central election commission so there's same voting all over the country. The United States lets every county decide basically how people vote with punch cards and that sort of thing. In other countries, we require that all of the qualified candidates have equal access to radio and television advertisement; whereas, in our country, we have to buy it. So, I would say that Citizens United ruling was a great setback to inherent democracy in our country, not just to the election process, but the entire gamut of democracy because it makes every successful electorate candidate in the Congress almost obligated to certain special interests for access and to answer their questions and to take advice on how to vote on crucial issues. I think it's been a terrible setback, and it's all recent.

KAYONGO: The next one is, "What recommendations, in addition to voting, do you have for ordinary citizens to change the discourse among elected officials in Washington, DC?"

CARTER: Well, along with that process has come the polarization of parties in Washington, DC. In addition to the massive infusion of money into the campaign that I've already covered, we also have gerrymandering. When a Republican or Democratic state legislature gets dominant, if the governor is the same party particularly, then they can contrive very complicated delineations of voting districts. Maybe in a certain state like Georgia, they want to put all the Black people in the same districts and let them have a few Black congressmen who are Democrats. Then the vast majority of the citizens, about 60 or 65 percent or so of being the other districts, and they're basically a Republican and white, so this is done all over the country. That's something that the Congress could change if they want to, but they don't because they have benefited from it, the ones in Congress now. But that's something that the Supreme Court could rule.

I think the Supreme Court could rule quite easily that there should be a blue-ribbon commission, for instance, of obviously balanced composition that would decide on the delineation of districts. I think two states have this requirement, and that's something that . . . So, gerrymandering, contriving districts, and the massive new addition of money has been the two worst things, and that has resulted in negative advertising. I never dreamed of having a negative commercial against one of my opponents for president. If I had, I would've been the one that people would've condemned, "You shouldn't cast aspersions on your opponent's character." Now that's where a lot of the money goes that you raise. You can raise all these millions of dollars and you spend them on commercials, and you try to tear down the reputation of your opponents, so that people get a bad impression of both candidates and then Republicans who begin to despise Democrats and vice versa.

When they get to Washington, they still despise each

other. So, you have almost 100 percent Republicans who will vote against anything President Obama asks for. So, the basic debates take place in the party caucuses. The Republicans all go to their caucus, and they decide how to vote, and then they almost have to vote 100 percent the way the majority says. We used to debate when I was president, but on the floor of the House and Senate, I should have long and very exciting debates to conclude a decision. That's no longer excellent. So, I'm being very critical of a political process and the government in my country, I feel that way. I don't apologize for it.

KAYONGO: This one puts you and I on the spot—

CARTER: Uh-oh. Read another one.

[*Laughter*]

CARTER: Go ahead. I'll try.

KAYONGO: It says, "Thank you for your call to action for the liberation and dignity for women. What is your message to men who don't think they're sexist, but who support language and policies that oppress women?"

CARTER: Well, I really would like for everybody who's interested in basic human rights or decency of moral values to read the book that I wrote about the oppression of women. It is the worst human rights crime on earth, and the people who perpetrate and enforce discrimination against women are basically men. A lot of these men are religious leaders, where early in my religion, happens to be Christianity, women were deacons and prophets and spiritual leaders of all kinds as expressed by St. Paul in his letters; he delineates, he gave the names of them. Then after a few years, though, within the Christian community, men became dominant and over a period of time, women are excluded from roles in churches, which gives a signal to everyone that in the eyes of God, men are superior, or women are inferior. If a woman can't be a deacon in the church, a woman can't be a chaplain, a woman can't be a priest, then this indicates that in the eyes of God, women are not qualified to be a deacon or a chaplain or a priest.

So, if a husband wants to dominate his wife or even abuse his wife, he says, "Well, if the church doesn't think my wife is equal to me, why should I treat her as an equal?" If an employer wants to cheat his women employees by paying her less than a man, they can say, maybe subconsciously, "If God doesn't think she's equal to me, why should I treat her as equal to my men workers?" So, you see, it permeates society, and also the element of violence; since I've already blamed the United Nations Security Council for encouraging or condoning violent acts instead of peace, this is also a factor in the abuse of women and girls, where dominant soldiers, primarily men, perpetrate horrible crimes of rape with bayonets and bottles and things of that kind. It's a horrible thing to talk about in some cases involving United Nations troops and involving troops from countries that volunteer to fight for the United Nations, so this is terrible. In my own country, Atlanta, Georgia, I would say is one of the most heavily trafficked places in our country in selling slaves.

AUDIENCE: Yes.

CARTER: We have the largest airport on earth, and a lot of our passengers come in from the Southern Hemisphere. A lot of the passengers brought in here are dark-skinned or African American, and they can be sold very cheaply to a brothel. The average price for a female sex worker is only $1,000. *The New York Times* did an analysis about a year ago or so that showed that a brothel owner can get $36,000 a year profit from her. So, there are between two and three hundred girls sold into slavery in Atlanta every month, and we have discrimination in our military forces as well. So, it's not just other countries that are guilty; it's our country as well. We know that we have a similar serious problem on college campuses with sexual abuse being prevalent and rarely, rarely even on the most enlightened campuses and outspoken at Harvard and Yale and Princeton, as well as other colleges, and they have a serious problem on those campuses as well. Rarely is a rapist on a college campus expelled.

The Justice Department says that over half of the sexual abuse on a campus is perpetrated by rapists, who once they get on a college campus, know that they can be satisfied by their sexual desires without punishment, with impunity, so they become habitual rapists. So, this is what we need to correct in our own country. In foreign countries, you have women whose sexual organs are abused with . . . horribly mutilated, and you have honor killings and other things, which our country's not guilty of, but it happens in every country around the world. So, it's the worst overall human rights abuse there is, and the men are responsible for it. It's the same thing that we had during the civil rights time. A lot of white people felt that discrimination or segregation was not right, but we benefited from it. We got the best jobs; we got the best education. We were the ones that determined the outcome of a jury case, so why should we give up this privilege even though we know it's wrong? Now men benefit from the discrimination against women, so why should we speak out about it? Why should we change the status quo that gives us a superior position in society? So, men are responsible, to answer your question. It's a long answer. I'm sorry.

KAYONGO: Yeah. Thank you. We have a few more before we close. This one is a little bit easier—

CARTER: Thank you.

KAYONGO: —and it's for the both of us. It talks about our upbringings. I find ourselves in an intersection. You have a little African boy over here from Uganda—

CARTER: Yeah, I want to hear about that.

KAYONGO: —who left the country as a former refugee during Idi Amin's time. And I landed in Kenya, where I grew up, and I was raised by an American woman from Pittsburgh, Marge Campbell. She's the one who taught me how to drink iced tea. Being British-raised, I was used to high tea—

CARTER: Sure.

KAYONGO: So, I thought she forgot to cook the tea.

[*Laughter*]

KAYONGO: Then she taught me how to eat cookies, and the British eat biscuits.

CARTER: Yes. Right.

KAYONGO: Now that I live here, I know that Americans give biscuits to dogs. Americans are so contrary.

CARTER: I also had biscuits for breakfast this morning.

KAYONGO: You have different kind of biscuits.

CARTER: Biscuits, yeah.

KAYONGO: It's a baked kind of thing.

CARTER: I understand that. Yeah.

KAYONGO: So, then I got to this country, and I checked into a hotel, and the hotel had three bars of soap: facial soap, hand washing soap, and body soap. What's the difference?

CARTER: I don't know. I don't know. I grew up with Octagon soap. I don't know if anybody has any of that. But I don't know the difference between the three soaps. I guess—

KAYONGO: Nothing.

CARTER: I guess it's a matter of—

KAYONGO: Marketing.

CARTER: —appealing or something.

KAYONGO: Marketing.

CARTER: Marketing, that's it. You sell more soap if you could get people to see there's three different kinds.

KAYONGO: But Americans are bougie like that. You know, they're—

CARTER: That's true. I don't disagree.

KAYONGO: So, then I end up [in] a good school up at Tufts, and I started the company, the Global Soap Project, that recycles all the soap, gives it to the Center for Disease Control and others who provide care to refugee camps back at home. Now, I find myself at the helm of the Center for Civil and Human Rights. That's my little story. What is your little story?

CARTER: Well, to start with soap, we used to make our own soap on the farm, and that was a big project that we had. Every time we killed hogs, we made soap. So, I grew up with a similar background to yours, but in a different part of the world.

KAYONGO: Yeah.

CARTER: Now I go into the hotels that have the soap. But as I said, as I said earlier, I think I was lucky that I just happened to grow up in a community that was African American. My mother was a registered nurse, and she was gone away a lot. She sometimes worked twenty-hour duty from two o'clock in the morning till ten o'clock at night. She only got off four hours a day, and she got paid ostensibly six dollars a day for twenty hours, so we didn't see my mother very much. So, I was basically raised by African American women. All my playmates were African American as well. So, I benefited ultimately from my mother's enlightened attitude toward the race issue, regardless of the morays and customs of the times. I think that's where I got my glimpse of what should be done about civil rights at home and human rights on a broad basis.

But I've seen the tremendous benefits that can come from opening up an opportunity for people to exhibit their human rights. One of the practical things was in South America. Before I was president, most of the countries in South America were military dictatorships. They were in bed with the presidents of the United States and with the corporations in the United States because they were the ones that controlled the iron ore and the bauxite and bananas and pineapples that came from there. To get a monopoly on those products was a great boon to our country and to our corporations who shared.

So, whenever one of those dictators was threatened by dissenting voices within his own country, from Indigenous Indians or from former slaves or from just poor people, the

United States would send troops down there to protect our friend, the dictator. So, in Colombia and Peru and Argentina and Chile and Brazil and Uruguay and Paraguay and so forth, from almost all those countries, we had military dictatorships. When I established a human rights policy and began to protect the rights of those poor and deprived and weak people to speak up, within ten years, every country in South America became a democracy. So, that's what I'm saying is, this is a practical indication of the benefits of just theoretically helping from a distance, for people to have a chance to speak their own mind and to elect their own leaders. So that's part of my background.

KAYONGO: So now I have two kids that I know of, at least.

CARTER: Yeah. I don't know what you mean by that, but—

KAYONGO: My wife is over there. Sorry, over there, and Kevin—

CARTER: Yes.

KAYONGO: —Kayongo is growing up as a new American. When I tell him, "Kevin, we are Africans"—

CARTER: How old is Kevin?

KAYONGO: Kevin is sixteen now.

CARTER: Okay.

KAYONGO: He's 6'4"—

CARTER: Wow.

KAYONGO: —and he plays basketball. He's a classically trained pianist.

CARTER: Oh, really? You should have brought him along.

KAYONGO: Yeah. I'm going to bring him next time.

CARTER: Bring him back. Okay?

KAYONGO: Then I have Lauren who is eleven.

CARTER: Yes.

KAYONGO: She's elegantly tough now, 'cause girls are different at that point. I love her to death. How do I take these two American kids and inspire them to understand that the country they live in is a remarkable country? Because we hear so much about the U.S. being a bad country and things are horrible and things are falling apart, how do we inspire hope right now?

CARTER: Well, I think there's a lot of reason for hope. Our country has learned the hard way, and a characteristic of America that gives me hope is the fact that we have such a heterogeneous population. The United States is not a melting pot; I think it's more of a mosaic where each individual still has a shining bright different color or different characteristic. When you put them all together, you have a group of courageous innovators that wanted to go to a foreign country to improve themselves or to demonstrate a commitment to a higher ideal, freedom of religion or whatever it was. So, we still have that inherent characteristic in our country. So, what we've had over now 230 years or so, is not only the ability but the proved commitment to improve ourselves. We make mistakes. But because we are a free society, our mistakes become increasingly apparent. We've already discussed some of them today. When those mistakes become adequately apparent to a majority of our people with a free voice in a democracy, they are self-correcting.

So, I think that's what gives us hope, and I've seen, and you've seen too, in the . . . less than half of my lifetime, I say since the 1960s, we've seen African Americans treated not only equally, but because of their superior quality in a superior way in basketball and baseball and football and so forth. So that has given the rest of society that is not interested in sports the realization that we all are equal in God's eyes and in our capabilities. So, some people have superior qualities in other stuff. So, I would say that your children, particularly 6'4" already, he's got a good future ahead of him. I think he'll probably get a scholarship in most colleges. I'm a trustee on a local college in Georgia. The college, by the way, is Mercer University. I'm a trustee now, but two years ago, Mercer with four thousand students beat Duke in basketball, so we can open the door for your son already. But I think there's plenty of opportunity for hope.

KAYONGO: Thank you. This one is from online. We have about three more of these. "Women earn less than men. How do you suggest we change this?" Or the second question you could tackle is, "Is it a right of an elected official to refuse to consider a Supreme Court nominee?" Take one of those.

CARTER: I think that the U.S. Senate Republicans have made a serious mistake in not considering the nominee for the Supreme Court that's been put forward by President Obama. They don't have to approve the very worthy candidate, but if the Judicial Committee would meet and say, "No," and then present the name to the Senate and they vote and say, "No," that would be okay with me. But I think to just refuse as though Obama was already out of office when he had almost a year to go, when the vote had occurred, I think that's wrong and a mistake. It doesn't violate the Constitution of the laws, but I think it violates the spirit of our country and sets a bad example for the future. So, I think I've answered that question adequately.

KAYONGO: Yeah. Well, let's talk about some concluding remarks.

CARTER: Okay.

KAYONGO: I'm inspired every day by different people. In the room today, we also have my board member at the Center for Civil and Human Rights and her husband. Andrea is Andrew Young's daughter.

CARTER: Andy Young's daughter?

KAYONGO: Yeah.

CARTER: Andrea. Which one?

KAYONGO: She's out there. Where is she? There she is. And her husband Jerry, right there.

CARTER: All right. You got a good boss then, Andrea.

KAYONGO: Every time I look at her, she inspires me. Who inspires you? What inspires you these days?

CARTER: Well, I was inspired by her father, and I still am. He set a moral and ethical standard for me as a president in dealing equitably with the people who lived in Africa. He did it in a quiet way without preaching to me, although he's a preacher, by his suggestion that we . . . And when Andy went on his first trip to Africa as my ambassador to the United Nations, he went there with this one purpose, that is to say, not what we want you to do, but what can the United States do for you? That was Andy's idea. He was gracious enough to give me credit for it, but it was his idea. So, there's still a lot of heroes that I have. Nelson Mandela was a great friend of mine. I was one of his intimate circle, and he's been to the Carter Center and he and I worked on human rights programs and other things. So, there are a lot of heroes still coming along. I'd say one, just to get . . . throw in, I started to say throw in a white person, but he is not white, and that was Anwar Sadat.

KAYONGO: Yeah.

CARTER: But he wasn't white either. But a white person who made a great impact on me was my early school superintendent, Mr. Coleman. I would say, Admiral Rickover, who was Jewish.

KAYONGO: Yes.

CARTER: Except for my mother and father, he had more influence on my life. So, we have plenty of heroes that we can look upon. So, we don't need to look very far for inspiration, but I happen to be religious, I believe, I think the ultimate standard of perfection for a human being is the life of Jesus Christ. That's what I teach in the Bible every Sunday morning in my little church. So, we can look at ancient times two thousand years ago. We can look in recent years and see people who've exhibited, with human courage and wisdom, the highest ideals that should guide us all.

KAYONGO: Well, before I thank you for what has been a wonderful and powerful hour with a seditious man of morality and kindness, I wanted to say you are my hero.

CARTER: Oh, thanks. Thank you. I appreciate it. I want to introduce . . . It's hard to see. Is Meredith Evans here?

KAYONGO: Right here.

AUDIENCE: Right here.

CARTER: Okay. Stand up again. You've been very busy.

KAYONGO: Yeah.

CARTER: Meredith, she's the director of our library museum and, of course, she's occupied a very important place in my life as well. I wanted to recognize her as well.

KAYONGO: Wow. Wow. That's awesome.

CARTER: Thank you, Meredith, very much. Thank you.

KAYONGO: Well, again, thank you so much for coming and being with us. We want to thank the museum for hosting us, Ambassador Peters for being with us, and for everyone here who's a distinguished guest and honored guest. Remember, these are wonderful moments. Treasure them and know that they don't come back. So, I wish there were more of us here to listen to a voice of perfection, President Carter.

CARTER: Thank you very much. I've enjoyed it. Thank you, everybody.

KAYONGO: So good for us to come out.

THE LAST INTERVIEW

INTERVIEW BY JUDY WOODRUFF
PBS
JULY 5, 2021

Jimmy and Rosalynn Carter reflect on seventy-five years of marriage, the state of American politics, July 5, 2021. Former first lady Rosalynn Carter is now ninety-three, and former President Jimmy Carter is ninety-six, making him the longest-living president in American history. This week, on July 7, marks their seventy-fifth wedding anniversary, another record among U.S. presidents. They sat down with Judy Woodruff in their hometown of Plains, Georgia, to discuss their life together, their legacy, and the current state of American politics.

JUDY WOODRUFF: It was the first Sunday in July of 1946. World War II had been over for months, and the victorious United States was emerging as a global superpower.

On that day, 140 miles south of Atlanta, in the small, quiet town of Plains, Georgia, a twenty-one-year-old recent Naval Academy graduate named James Earl Carter, Jr., and his eighteen-year-old fiancée, Eleanor Rosalynn Smith, exchanged wedding vows. They walked down the aisle of a Methodist church and into a partnership that would take them to the height of American power and all over the world.

Former first lady Rosalynn Carter is now ninety-three, and former President Jimmy Carter is ninety-six, making him the longest-living president in American history.

This Wednesday, July 7, marks their seventy-fifth wedding anniversary, another record among U.S. presidents. And it was for that occasion that I spoke with them last week in Plains, where they still live, about their life together and a few other things.

WOODRUFF: President Carter, Mrs. Carter, it is so wonderful to see both of you. Thank you for talking with us.

Seventy-five years of marriage, that is remarkable. Congratulations. Mrs. Carter, what is the secret to this partnership?

ROSALYNN CARTER: Well, I think we give each other space and we try to do things together. We're always looking for things we can do together, like birding and fly-fishing and just anything we can find to do together.

WOODRUFF: And, President Carter, I think people look at this long and happy marriage, and I think they'd love to know what—especially couples who have been through what the two of you have been through—what's the secret, when you don't see eye to eye on something, for how you patch it back together?

JIMMY CARTER: At the end of the day, we try to become reconciled and overcome all the differences that arose during the day. We also make up and give each other a kiss before we go to sleep, still in bed. And we always read the Bible every night, which adds a different aspect to life. So, we really try to become completely reconciled each night before we go to sleep.

WOODRUFF: I'm asking about that, Mrs. Carter, because the story is, when you were writing your book together, it was difficult for the two of you to work together.

MRS. CARTER: It was not easy. It's the worst thing—I mean, it's probably the closest thing to bringing us to a divorce that we ever did. It was awful.

WOODRUFF: But you got through it.

MRS. CARTER: We got through it. But we had help, and say, Mrs. Carter, you do—you say this, and President Carter, you say this. And—but we got through it.

WOODRUFF: And to those Americans who see the both of you and want to know, how are you doing, what would you say, Mrs. Carter?

MRS. CARTER: Doing good. We're doing good, both of us.

WOODRUFF: And President Carter?

CARTER: Well, we raise a lot. And I swim three times a day and I walk every day.

MRS. CARTER: Every day.

CARTER: And so, we stay in good physical shape, as best we can, with our handicaps. And we have had to live a quite restricted life the last year or so with the problem with the virus. But we have succeeded very well. And I think, in general, that handicap in movement has brought us even closer together. So that's one thing for which I'm thankful.

WOODRUFF: And, President Carter, you have now lived long enough to see this reevaluation of your presidency. There are two new major biographies out that argue that you didn't get the credit that you deserved for so much of what you did as president, whether it was climate change, energy, human rights, the Camp David Accords, the Panama Canal treaties.

How do you look on what's going on right now with your presidency?

CARTER: Well, I'm glad to know that people are now remembering that, during my administration, we tried to keep the peace. And we cherished our human rights. So, peace and human rights were the bases for my campaign, and also my administration. So, we came out of the White House completely satisfied with the way we had acted in the trials that we made to overcome difficulties. And most of the time, we succeeded. At least we thought we did.

WOODRUFF: And, Mrs. Carter, when you look at this reevaluation, if that's what you want to call it, I mean, how do you see it? Is it about time? Is it—how do you think about it?

MRS. CARTER: I think it's about time that people really realize what Jimmy did. And the books are helping. And I have been pleased with that.

WOODRUFF: So, President Carter, there's so much to ask you both about. But, as you think back on your presidency and your time as a former president, what are you most proud of? Is there a big regret you have?

CARTER: Well, we're very proud of having been elected and having served as president. That's the epitome of our lives, I think, in totality. And I would say that we did what we pledged to do in the campaign. We kept the peace, and we obeyed the law, and we told the truth, and we honored human rights. Those were things that were important to me.

WOODRUFF: And during your presidency, there was clearly a big partisan divide in this country. There were disagreements with Republicans, certainly with President Reagan in that campaign of 1980. But, today, the partisanship is—just seems to be off the charts. It's hyper partisan. Do you think you could have done what you did as president if—in this environment?

CARTER: No. If the Republicans had pledged while I was president not ever to pass any of my bills, I would have been handicapped greatly. And I'm glad they didn't do that. But we had a very good batting average with the Congress when I was in office. I think we had the best one since Lyndon Johnson did. So, we had a good administration.

WOODRUFF: And, Mrs. Carter, as you think about the partisanship of today and the—certainly, you had—there were difficult moments during your presidency in getting done what you wanted to get done. But, today, you not only have partisanship. You have a president who claims that he won an election that he didn't. You have millions and millions of Americans, including here in Georgia, who say that President Trump won reelection. How do you absorb that?

MRS. CARTER: It's hard. It's hard for me to know what was happening, and then to hear what was being said about it. And . . .

CARTER: It's known, quite accurately, as the big lie. And how he—how Trump gets away with it is hard to comprehend. And this is a time for extreme partnership—partisanship. I think that adds to the environment within which a big lie would be possible to sustain.

WOODRUFF: Do you believe that—what would you say to Georgians, your fellow Georgians, so many of whom believe that President Trump won? And the laws have now been changed in the state of Georgia that might have made it difficult for President Biden or Senator Warnock or Senator Ossoff to win?

CARTER: Well, we have a few of those people in Plains, unfortunately. But I don't think they—I'm going to change their mind. They're convinced of a lie. And they're going to maintain it until they're gone, perhaps. So, we just have to live with that and accommodate other people what they believe, and not be overly critical of them.

WOODRUFF: Did you ever think, Mrs. Carter, that your own Carter Center would be involved in monitoring elections in Georgia? You have monitored elections all over the world, over a hundred of them, and you're now involved in monitoring elections in this country.

MRS. CARTER: In this state? No, I never thought we would have to monitor elections in Georgia. I just assumed elections were accurate. And I trusted our officials. Looking back on it, it's not a very good thing I did, but I did. I trusted the officials. And I still do, to some extent. I think we know the ones that don't tell the truth and try to—well, I don't call it corrupt . . . corruption because I don't think that's a good definition for it.

WOODRUFF: And they're monitoring—President Carter, they're monitoring for fraud. They're also monitoring for access to make sure people who should be able to vote can vote. How—I mean, how concerned are you with, again, the fact that your own Carter Center is now involved in this?

CARTER: I think, all over the world, we have always, ever since the Carter Center was founded, tried to promote maximum involvement among the people in the election itself and make sure that votes were counted accurately. And all those things have gone by the board because of a Republican state legislature who take the position that Trump has espoused. So, I think we will just have to grin and bear it until the time comes when it changes, which I hope will be soon.

WOODRUFF: President Biden, you have known him a very

long time. He was the first United States senator to endorse you when you ran for president.

CARTER: I remember.

WOODRUFF: How is he doing? We're almost six months in. What are his main challenges now? How's he doing?

CARTER: Well, the immigration question still has arisen. And I don't think we have still worked out an accommodation with China that's satisfactory for the long term. And the legislative—legislation that he wants to do is still under discussion. We don't know how it's going to turn out. But I think that, in general, Joe Biden has done very well.

WOODRUFF: And, Mrs. Carter, what do you think his main challenges are?

MRS. CARTER: I think it's a great relief to have Joe Biden in office, after what we had before, so I'm very pleased about it.

WOODRUFF: Two things I want to specifically ask both of you, and, Mrs. Carter, to you first.
    Mental health has been a primary interest to you. You have poured a lot of energy into it. And we have seen, with the pandemic, it's underlined how difficult mental and emotional health is for many Americans. What is the one thing you would like to see the federal government do to improve Americans' ability to get the help they need?

MRS. CARTER: I think that making a big issue out of it would help, because I worked very hard trying to remove the stigma of mental illness. And I think that one thing that has happened is that the situation has changed, that a little bit, done away a little bit with the stigma. I have been pleased to see that. I think more people are seeking help than they did in the past.

And I just hope that people will know that they don't have to suffer from mental illnesses. The treatment—there's treatment now. Everybody can live a good life in their communities, working and living a normal life with a mental illness.

WOODRUFF: And, President Carter, I want to ask you to look ahead. As you think about your grandchildren and your great-grandchildren and their future in this country, are you fearful for the United States, or are you more hopeful?

CARTER: Well, sometimes I'm fearful and sometimes I'm hopeful. But, overwhelmingly, I'm hopeful. I have confidence in the basic integrity of the American people as—in totality. And I believe that we have overcome even worse and more serious problems in the past than we have to face today. And so, in looking at the historical paths of America, I still have ultimate hope in the American people.

WOODRUFF: How do you see that, Mrs. Carter?

MRS. CARTER: I think that's a good answer. I think you have to have hope. Sometimes it's hard, with the issues and the things that are on the news all the time, to try to figure out what's really—what really to believe. But, in the end, I think everything will be OK.

CARTER: We watch the *NewsHour*, and your leadership and assessment every night. And that kind of helps to reassure us. And I think we don't watch FOX's presentations very much. We watch MSNBC and CNN very rarely. And all the aspects of social media, we don't really become involved in it. So, we have a very good balance of news coverage. So, I think, with Biden in office and with the inherent qualities of the American people's judgment, I would say I'm fairly optimistic about the future.

WOODRUFF: Well, we are very grateful to both of you for talking with us today, and on the occasion of your seventy-fifth wedding anniversary. Congratulations on that. It's really wonderful to see both of you. Thank you very much.

CARTER: We appreciate you. Thank you.

JAMES EARL CARTER JR. came from a background of farming and military service to forge an unlikely political career, first as governor of Georgia, and then as the 39th president of the United States. Once out of office he embarked on a remarkable second career as a citizen diplomat of history-making ability and as the founder of numerous charity and philanthropic organizations. Jimmy Carter was awarded the Nobel Peace Prize in 2002.

WILLIAM F. BUCKLEY JR. was the founder of the iconic conservative journal the *National Review* and of *Firing Line*, the televised interview program he hosted from 1966 to 1999. He was the author of the UPI syndicated column "On the Right" as well as the books *God and Man at Yale* and *McCarthy and His Enemies*.

WIL S. HYLTON has been a contributing writer for the *New York Times Magazine* and has published cover stories for the *New Yorker, Rolling Stone, Esquire, Harper's, Details, GQ,* and many others. He is the recipient of the John Bartlow Martin Award for Public Interest Journalism from the Medill School of Journalism.

DERRECK KAYONGO is an entrepreneur and human rights innovator born in Kampala, Uganda, just before General Idi Amin Dada seized power in a military coup. As violence spread through the country and civil war erupted, Kayongo and his family became refugees in Kenya before immigrating to the United States. Kayongo is the former director of the National Center for Human and Civil Rights and a renowned

TEDx speaker whose speeches have been viewed by, and an inspiration to, millions.

JIM LEHRER was the executive editor and a news anchor for *PBS NewsHour* and was known for his role as a debate moderator during US presidential election campaigns, moderating twelve presidential debates between 1988 and 2012. He has been the recipient of many awards, including the George Foster Peabody Broadcast Award, the William Allen White Foundation Award for Journalistic Merit, and the University of Missouri School of Journalism's Medal of Honor.

ROBERT SCHEER was a national correspondent at the *Los Angeles Times* for seventeen years and a contributing editor at *The Nation* magazine, as well as a founding editor in chief of the award-winning online newsmagazine *Truthdig*. Scheer was a contributing script consultant for the 1995 film *Nixon*, directed by Oliver Stone.

JUDY WOODRUFF is an American broadcast journalist who worked in local, network, cable, and public television news since 1970. She was the anchor and managing editor of *PBS NewsHour* from 2013 to 2022, and has covered every presidential election and convention since 1976. Among her many awards are the Peabody Award for Journalistic Integrity, the Walter Cronkite Award for Excellence in Journalism, and International Matrix Award from the Association for Women in Communications.